Mometrix
TEST PREPARATION

Regents

Success Strategies
Living Environment

I0883724

Dear Future Exam Success Story

First of all, **THANK YOU** for purchasing Mometrix study materials!

Second, congratulations! You are one of the few determined test-takers who are committed to doing whatever it takes to excel on your exam. **You have come to the right place.** We developed these study materials with one goal in mind: to deliver you the information you need in a format that's concise and easy to use.

In addition to optimizing your guide for the content of the test, we've outlined our recommended steps for breaking down the preparation process into small, attainable goals so you can make sure you stay on track.

We've also analyzed the entire test-taking process, identifying the most common pitfalls and showing how you can overcome them and be ready for any curveball the test throws you.

Standardized testing is one of the biggest obstacles on your road to success, which only increases the importance of doing well in the high-pressure, high-stakes environment of test day. Your results on this test could have a significant impact on your future, and this guide provides the information and practical advice to help you achieve your full potential on test day.

Your success is our success

We would love to hear from you! If you would like to share the story of your exam success or if you have any questions or comments in regard to our products, please contact us at **800-673-8175** or **support@mometrix.com**.

Thanks again for your business and we wish you continued success!

Sincerely,
The Mometrix Test Preparation Team

Printed in the United States of America

TABLE OF CONTENTS

Introduction

Thank you for purchasing this resource! You have made the choice to prepare yourself for a test that could have a huge impact on your future, and this guide is designed to help you be fully ready for test day. Obviously, it's important to have a solid understanding of the test material, but you also need to be prepared for the unique environment and stressors of the test, so that you can perform to the best of your abilities.

For this purpose, the first section that appears in this guide is the **Success Strategies**. We've devoted countless hours to meticulously researching what works and what doesn't, and we've boiled down our findings to the five most impactful steps you can take to improve your performance on the test. We start at the beginning with study planning and move through the preparation process, all the way to the testing strategies that will help you get the most out of what you know when you're finally sitting in front of the test.

We recommend that you start preparing for your test as far in advance as possible. However, if you've bought this guide as a last-minute study resource and only have a few days before your test, we recommend that you skip over the first two Success Strategies since they address a long-term study plan.

If you struggle with **test anxiety**, we strongly encourage you to check out our recommendations for how you can overcome it. Test anxiety is a formidable foe, but it can be beaten, and we want to make sure you have the tools you need to defeat it.

Strategy #1 – Plan Big, Study Small

There's a lot riding on your performance. If you want to ace this test, you're going to need to keep your skills sharp and the material fresh in your mind. You need a plan that lets you review everything you need to know while still fitting in your schedule. We'll break this strategy down into three categories.

Information Organization

Start with the information you already have: the official test outline. From this, you can make a complete list of all the concepts you need to cover before the test. Organize these concepts into groups that can be studied together, and create a list of any related vocabulary you need to learn so you can brush up on any difficult terms. You'll want to keep this vocabulary list handy once you actually start studying since you may need to add to it along the way.

Time Management

Once you have your set of study concepts, decide how to spread them out over the time you have left before the test. Break your study plan into small, clear goals so you have a manageable task for each day and know exactly what you're doing. Then just focus on one small step at a time. When you manage your time this way, you don't need to spend hours at a time studying. Studying a small block of content for a short period each day helps you retain information better and avoid stressing over how much you have left to do. You can relax knowing that you have a plan to cover everything in time. In order for this strategy to be effective though, you have to start studying early and stick to your schedule. Avoid the exhaustion and futility that comes from last-minute cramming!

Study Environment

The environment you study in has a big impact on your learning. Studying in a coffee shop, while probably more enjoyable, is not likely to be as fruitful as studying in a quiet room. It's important to keep distractions to a minimum. You're only planning to study for a short block of time, so make the most of it. Don't pause to check your phone or get up to find a snack. It's also important to **avoid multitasking**. Research has consistently shown that multitasking will make your studying dramatically less effective. Your study area should also be comfortable and well-lit so you don't have the distraction of straining your eyes or sitting on an uncomfortable chair.

The time of day you study is also important. You want to be rested and alert. Don't wait until just before bedtime. Study when you'll be most likely to comprehend and remember. Even better, if you know what time of day your test will be, set that time aside for study. That way your brain will be used to working on that subject at that specific time and you'll have a better chance of recalling information.

Finally, it can be helpful to team up with others who are studying for the same test. Your actual studying should be done in as isolated an environment as possible, but the work of organizing the information and setting up the study plan can be divided up. In between study sessions, you can discuss with your teammates the concepts that you're all studying and quiz each other on the details. Just be sure that your teammates are as serious about the test as you are. If you find that your study time is being replaced with social time, you might need to find a new team.

Strategy #2 – Make Your Studying Count

You're devoting a lot of time and effort to preparing for this test, so you want to be absolutely certain it will pay off. This means doing more than just reading the content and hoping you can remember it on test day. It's important to make every minute of study count. There are two main areas you can focus on to make your studying count.

Retention

It doesn't matter how much time you study if you can't remember the material. You need to make sure you are retaining the concepts. To check your retention of the information you're learning, try recalling it at later times with minimal prompting. Try carrying around flashcards and glance at one or two from time to time or ask a friend who's also studying for the test to quiz you.

To enhance your retention, look for ways to put the information into practice so that you can apply it rather than simply recalling it. If you're using the information in practical ways, it will be much easier to remember. Similarly, it helps to solidify a concept in your mind if you're not only reading it to yourself but also explaining it to someone else. Ask a friend to let you teach them about a concept you're a little shaky on (or speak aloud to an imaginary audience if necessary). As you try to summarize, define, give examples, and answer your friend's questions, you'll understand the concepts better and they will stay with you longer. Finally, step back for a big picture view and ask yourself how each piece of information fits with the whole subject. When you link the different concepts together and see them working together as a whole, it's easier to remember the individual components.

Finally, practice showing your work on any multi-step problems, even if you're just studying. Writing out each step you take to solve a problem will help solidify the process in your mind, and you'll be more likely to remember it during the test.

Modality

Modality simply refers to the means or method by which you study. Choosing a study modality that fits your own individual learning style is crucial. No two people learn best in exactly the same way, so it's important to know your strengths and use them to your advantage.

For example, if you learn best by visualization, focus on visualizing a concept in your mind and draw an image or a diagram. Try color-coding your notes, illustrating them, or creating symbols that will trigger your mind to recall a learned concept. If you learn best by hearing or discussing information, find a study partner who learns the same way or read aloud to yourself. Think about how to put the information in your own words. Imagine that you are giving a lecture on the topic and record yourself so you can listen to it later.

For any learning style, flashcards can be helpful. Organize the information so you can take advantage of spare moments to review. Underline key words or phrases. Use different colors for different categories. Mnemonic devices (such as creating a short list in which every item starts with the same letter) can also help with retention. Find what works best for you and use it to store the information in your mind most effectively and easily.

Strategy #3 – Practice the Right Way

Your success on test day depends not only on how many hours you put into preparing, but also on whether you prepared the right way. It's good to check along the way to see if your studying is paying off. One of the most effective ways to do this is by taking practice tests to evaluate your progress. Practice tests are useful because they show exactly where you need to improve. Every time you take a practice test, pay special attention to these three groups of questions:

- The questions you got wrong
- The questions you had to guess on, even if you guessed right
- The questions you found difficult or slow to work through

This will show you exactly what your weak areas are, and where you need to devote more study time. Ask yourself why each of these questions gave you trouble. Was it because you didn't understand the material? Was it because you didn't remember the vocabulary? Do you need more repetitions on this type of question to build speed and confidence? Dig into those questions and figure out how you can strengthen your weak areas as you go back to review the material.

Additionally, many practice tests have a section explaining the answer choices. It can be tempting to read the explanation and think that you now have a good understanding of the concept. However, an explanation likely only covers part of the question's broader context. Even if the explanation makes perfect sense, **go back and investigate** every concept related to the question until you're positive you have a thorough understanding.

As you go along, keep in mind that the practice test is just that: practice. Memorizing these questions and answers will not be very helpful on the actual test because it is unlikely to have any of the same exact questions. If you only know the right answers to the sample questions, you won't be prepared for the real thing. **Study the concepts** until you understand them fully, and then you'll be able to answer any question that shows up on the test.

It's important to wait on the practice tests until you're ready. If you take a test on your first day of study, you may be overwhelmed by the amount of material covered and how much you need to learn. Work up to it gradually.

On test day, you'll need to be prepared for answering questions, managing your time, and using the test-taking strategies you've learned. It's a lot to balance, like a mental marathon that will have a big impact on your future. Like training for a marathon, you'll need to start slowly and work your way up. When test day arrives, you'll be ready.

Start with the strategies you've read in the first two Success Strategies—plan your course and study in the way that works best for you. If you have time, consider using multiple study resources to get different approaches to the same concepts. It can be helpful to see difficult concepts from more than one angle. Then find a good source for practice tests. Many times, the test website will suggest potential study resources or provide sample tests.

Practice Test Strategy

If you're able to find at least three practice tests, we recommend this strategy:

Untimed and Open-Book Practice

Take the first test with no time constraints and with your notes and study guide handy. Take your time and focus on applying the strategies you've learned.

Timed and Open-Book Practice

Take the second practice test open-book as well, but set a timer and practice pacing yourself to finish in time.

Timed and Closed-Book Practice

Take any other practice tests as if it were test day. Set a timer and put away your study materials. Sit at a table or desk in a quiet room, imagine yourself at the testing center, and answer questions as quickly and accurately as possible.

Keep repeating timed and closed-book tests on a regular basis until you run out of practice tests or it's time for the actual test. Your mind will be ready for the schedule and stress of test day, and you'll be able to focus on recalling the material you've learned.

Strategy #4 – Pace Yourself

Once you're fully prepared for the material on the test, your biggest challenge on test day will be managing your time. Just knowing that the clock is ticking can make you panic even if you have plenty of time left. Work on pacing yourself so you can build confidence against the time constraints of the exam. Pacing is a difficult skill to master, especially in a high-pressure environment, so **practice is vital**.

Set time expectations for your pace based on how much time is available. For example, if a section has 60 questions and the time limit is 30 minutes, you know you have to average 30 seconds or less per question in order to answer them all. Although 30 seconds is the hard limit, set 25 seconds per question as your goal, so you reserve extra time to spend on harder questions. When you budget extra time for the harder questions, you no longer have any reason to stress when those questions take longer to answer.

Don't let this time expectation distract you from working through the test at a calm, steady pace, but keep it in mind so you don't spend too much time on any one question. Recognize that taking extra time on one question you don't understand may keep you from answering two that you do understand later in the test. If your time limit for a question is up and you're still not sure of the answer, mark it and move on, and come back to it later if the time and the test format allow. If the testing format doesn't allow you to return to earlier questions, just make an educated guess; then put it out of your mind and move on.

On the easier questions, be careful not to rush. It may seem wise to hurry through them so you have more time for the challenging ones, but it's not worth missing one if you know the concept and just didn't take the time to read the question fully. Work efficiently but make sure you understand the question and have looked at all of the answer choices, since more than one may seem right at first.

Even if you're paying attention to the time, you may find yourself a little behind at some point. You should speed up to get back on track, but do so wisely. Don't panic; just take a few seconds less on each question until you're caught up. Don't guess without thinking, but do look through the answer choices and eliminate any you know are wrong. If you can get down to two choices, it is often worthwhile to guess from those. Once you've chosen an answer, move on and don't dwell on any that you skipped or had to hurry through. If a question was taking too long, chances are it was one of the harder ones, so you weren't as likely to get it right anyway.

On the other hand, if you find yourself getting ahead of schedule, it may be beneficial to slow down a little. The more quickly you work, the more likely you are to make a careless mistake that will affect your score. You've budgeted time for each question, so don't be afraid to spend that time. Practice an efficient but careful pace to get the most out of the time you have.

Test-Taking Strategies

This section contains a list of test-taking strategies that you may find helpful as you work through the test. By taking what you know and applying logical thought, you can maximize your chances of answering any question correctly!

It is very important to realize that every question is different and every person is different: no single strategy will work on every question, and no single strategy will work for every person. That's why we've included all of them here, so you can try them out and determine which ones work best for different types of questions and which ones work best for you.

Question Strategies

⊘ Read Carefully

Read the question and the answer choices carefully. Don't miss the question because you misread the terms. You have plenty of time to read each question thoroughly and make sure you understand what is being asked. Yet a happy medium must be attained, so don't waste too much time. You must read carefully and efficiently.

⊘ Contextual Clues

Look for contextual clues. If the question includes a word you are not familiar with, look at the immediate context for some indication of what the word might mean. Contextual clues can often give you all the information you need to decipher the meaning of an unfamiliar word. Even if you can't determine the meaning, you may be able to narrow down the possibilities enough to make a solid guess at the answer to the question.

⊘ Prefixes

If you're having trouble with a word in the question or answer choices, try dissecting it. Take advantage of every clue that the word might include. Prefixes can be a huge help. Usually, they allow you to determine a basic meaning. *Pre-* means before, *post-* means after, *pro-* is positive, *de-* is negative. From prefixes, you can get an idea of the general meaning of the word and try to put it into context.

⊘ Hedge Words

Watch out for critical hedge words, such as *likely, may, can, often, almost, mostly, usually, generally, rarely*, and *sometimes*. Question writers insert these hedge phrases to cover every possibility. Often an answer choice will be wrong simply because it leaves no room for exception. Be on guard for answer choices that have definitive words such as *exactly* and *always*.

⊘ Switchback Words

Stay alert for *switchbacks*. These are the words and phrases frequently used to alert you to shifts in thought. The most common switchback words are *but, although*, and *however*. Others include *nevertheless, on the other hand, even though, while, in spite of, despite*, and *regardless of*. Switchback words are important to catch because they can change the direction of the question or an answer choice.

✓ Face Value

When in doubt, use common sense. Accept the situation in the problem at face value. Don't read too much into it. These problems will not require you to make wild assumptions. If you have to go beyond creativity and warp time or space in order to have an answer choice fit the question, then you should move on and consider the other answer choices. These are normal problems rooted in reality. The applicable relationship or explanation may not be readily apparent, but it is there for you to figure out. Use your common sense to interpret anything that isn't clear.

Answer Choice Strategies

✓ Answer Selection

The most thorough way to pick an answer choice is to identify and eliminate wrong answers until only one is left, then confirm it is the correct answer. Sometimes an answer choice may immediately seem right, but be careful. The test writers will usually put more than one reasonable answer choice on each question, so take a second to read all of them and make sure that the other choices are not equally obvious. As long as you have time left, it is better to read every answer choice than to pick the first one that looks right without checking the others.

✓ Answer Choice Families

An answer choice family consists of two (in rare cases, three) answer choices that are very similar in construction and cannot all be true at the same time. If you see two answer choices that are direct opposites or parallels, one of them is usually the correct answer. For instance, if one answer choice says that quantity *x* increases and another either says that quantity *x* decreases (opposite) or says that quantity *y* increases (parallel), then those answer choices would fall into the same family. An answer choice that doesn't match the construction of the answer choice family is more likely to be incorrect. Most questions will not have answer choice families, but when they do appear, you should be prepared to recognize them.

✓ Eliminate Answers

Eliminate answer choices as soon as you realize they are wrong, but make sure you consider all possibilities. If you are eliminating answer choices and realize that the last one you are left with is also wrong, don't panic. Start over and consider each choice again. There may be something you missed the first time that you will realize on the second pass.

✓ Avoid Fact Traps

Don't be distracted by an answer choice that is factually true but doesn't answer the question. You are looking for the choice that answers the question. Stay focused on what the question is asking for so you don't accidentally pick an answer that is true but incorrect. Always go back to the question and make sure the answer choice you've selected actually answers the question and is not merely a true statement.

✓ Extreme Statements

In general, you should avoid answers that put forth extreme actions as standard practice or proclaim controversial ideas as established fact. An answer choice that states the "process should be used in certain situations, if..." is much more likely to be correct than one that states the "process should be discontinued completely." The first is a calm rational statement and doesn't even make a definitive, uncompromising stance, using a hedge word *if* to provide wiggle room, whereas the second choice is far more extreme.

⊘ Benchmark

As you read through the answer choices and you come across one that seems to answer the question well, mentally select that answer choice. This is not your final answer, but it's the one that will help you evaluate the other answer choices. The one that you selected is your benchmark or standard for judging each of the other answer choices. Every other answer choice must be compared to your benchmark. That choice is correct until proven otherwise by another answer choice beating it. If you find a better answer, then that one becomes your new benchmark. Once you've decided that no other choice answers the question as well as your benchmark, you have your final answer.

⊘ Predict the Answer

Before you even start looking at the answer choices, it is often best to try to predict the answer. When you come up with the answer on your own, it is easier to avoid distractions and traps because you will know exactly what to look for. The right answer choice is unlikely to be word-for-word what you came up with, but it should be a close match. Even if you are confident that you have the right answer, you should still take the time to read each option before moving on.

General Strategies

⊘ Tough Questions

If you are stumped on a problem or it appears too hard or too difficult, don't waste time. Move on! Remember though, if you can quickly check for obviously incorrect answer choices, your chances of guessing correctly are greatly improved. Before you completely give up, at least try to knock out a couple of possible answers. Eliminate what you can and then guess at the remaining answer choices before moving on.

⊘ Check Your Work

Since you will probably not know every term listed and the answer to every question, it is important that you get credit for the ones that you do know. Don't miss any questions through careless mistakes. If at all possible, try to take a second to look back over your answer selection and make sure you've selected the correct answer choice and haven't made a costly careless mistake (such as marking an answer choice that you didn't mean to mark). This quick double check should more than pay for itself in caught mistakes for the time it costs.

⊘ Pace Yourself

It's easy to be overwhelmed when you're looking at a page full of questions; your mind is confused and full of random thoughts, and the clock is ticking down faster than you would like. Calm down and maintain the pace that you have set for yourself. Especially as you get down to the last few minutes of the test, don't let the small numbers on the clock make you panic. As long as you are on track by monitoring your pace, you are guaranteed to have time for each question.

⊘ Don't Rush

It is very easy to make errors when you are in a hurry. Maintaining a fast pace in answering questions is pointless if it makes you miss questions that you would have gotten right otherwise. Test writers like to include distracting information and wrong answers that seem right. Taking a little extra time to avoid careless mistakes can make all the difference in your test score. Find a pace that allows you to be confident in the answers that you select.

⊘ KEEP MOVING

Panicking will not help you pass the test, so do your best to stay calm and keep moving. Taking deep breaths and going through the answer elimination steps you practiced can help to break through a stress barrier and keep your pace.

Final Notes

The combination of a solid foundation of content knowledge and the confidence that comes from practicing your plan for applying that knowledge is the key to maximizing your performance on test day. As your foundation of content knowledge is built up and strengthened, you'll find that the strategies included in this chapter become more and more effective in helping you quickly sift through the distractions and traps of the test to isolate the correct answer.

Now that you're preparing to move forward into the test content chapters of this book, be sure to keep your goal in mind. As you read, think about how you will be able to apply this information on the test. If you've already seen sample questions for the test and you have an idea of the question format and style, try to come up with questions of your own that you can answer based on what you're reading. This will give you valuable practice applying your knowledge in the same ways you can expect to on test day.

Good luck and good studying!

Scientific Process

Safety and Equipment

Laboratory Accidents

Any spills or accidents should be **reported** to the teacher so that the teacher can determine the safest clean-up method. The student should start to wash off a **chemical** spilled on the skin while reporting the incident. Some spills may require removal of contaminated clothing and use of the **safety shower**. Broken glass should be disposed of in a designated container. If someone's clothing catches fire they should walk to the safety shower and use it to extinguish the flames. A fire blanket may be used to smother a **lab fire**. A fire extinguisher, phone, spill neutralizers, and a first aid box are other types of **safety equipment** found in the lab. Students should be familiar with **routes** out of the room and the building in case of fire. Students should use the **eye wash station** if a chemical gets in the eyes.

Safety Procedures

Students should wear a **lab apron** and **safety goggles**. Loose or dangling clothing and jewelry, necklaces, and earrings should not be worn. Those with long hair should tie it back. Care should always be taken not to splash chemicals. Open-toed shoes such as sandals and flip-flops should not be worn, nor should wrist watches. Glasses are preferable to contact lenses since the latter carry a risk of chemicals getting caught between the lens and the eye. Students should always be supervised. The area where the experiment is taking place and the surrounding floor should be free of clutter. Only the lab book and the items necessary for the experiment should be present. Smoking, eating, and chewing gum are not permitted in the lab. Cords should not be allowed to dangle from work stations. There should be no rough-housing in the lab. Hands should be washed after the lab is complete.

Fume Hoods

Because of the potential safety hazards associated with chemistry lab experiments, such as fire from vapors and the inhalation of toxic fumes, a **fume hood** should be used in many instances. A fume hood carries away vapors from reagents or reactions. Equipment or reactions are placed as far back in the hood as practical to help enhance the collection of the fumes. The **glass safety shield** automatically closes to the appropriate height, and it should be low enough to protect the face and body. The safety shield should only be raised to move equipment in and out of the hood. One should not climb inside a hood or stick one's head inside. All spills should be wiped up immediately, and the glass should be cleaned if a splash occurs.

Common Safety Hazards

Some specific safety hazards possible in a chemistry lab include:

- **Fire**: Fire can be caused by volatile solvents such as ether, acetone, or benzene being kept in an open beaker or Erlenmeyer flask. Vapors can creep along the table and ignite if they reach a flame or spark. Solvents should be heated in a hood with a steam bath, not on a hot plate.
- **Explosion**: Heating or creating a reaction in a closed system can cause an explosion, resulting in flying glass and chemical splashes. The system should be vented to prevent this.
- **Chemical and thermal burns**: Many chemicals are corrosive to the skin and eyes.

- **Inhalation of toxic fumes**: Some compounds severely irritate membranes in the eyes, nose, throat, and lungs.
- **Absorption** of toxic chemicals such as dimethyl sulfoxide (DMSO) and nitrobenzene through the skin.
- **Ingestion** of toxic chemicals.

Safety Gloves

There are many types of **gloves** available to help protect the skin from cuts, burns, and chemical splashes. There are many considerations when choosing a glove. For example, gloves that are highly protective may limit dexterity. Some gloves may not offer appropriate protection against a specific chemical. Other considerations include degradation rating, which indicates how effective a glove is when exposed to chemicals; breakthrough time, which indicates how quickly a chemical can break through the surface of the glove; and permeation rate, which indicates how quickly chemicals seep through after the initial breakthrough. Disposable latex, vinyl, or nitrile gloves are usually appropriate for most circumstances, and offer protection from incidental splashes and contact. Other types of gloves include butyl, neoprene, PVC, PVA, Viton, Silver Shield, and natural rubber. Each offers its own type of protection but may have drawbacks as well.

Proper Handling and Storage of Chemicals

Students should take care when **carrying chemicals** from one place to another. Chemicals should never be taken from the room, tasted, or touched with bare hands. **Safety gloves** should be worn when appropriate and glove/chemical interactions and glove deterioration should be considered. Hands should always be **washed** thoroughly after a lab. Potentially hazardous materials intended for use in chemistry, biology, or other science labs should be secured in a safe area where relevant **Safety Data Sheets (SDS)** can be accessed. Chemicals and solutions should be used as directed and labels should be read before handling solutions and chemicals. Extra chemicals should not be returned to their original containers, but should be disposed of as directed by the school district's rules or local ordinances. Local municipalities often have hazardous waste disposal programs. Acids should be stored separately from other chemicals. Flammable liquids should be stored away from acids, bases, and oxidizers.

Bunsen Burners

When using a **Bunsen burner**, loose clothing should be tucked in, long hair should be tied back, and safety goggles and aprons should be worn. Students should know what to do in case of a fire or accident. When lighting the burner, strikers should always be used instead of matches. Do not touch the hot barrel. Tongs (never fingers) should be used to hold the material in the flame. To heat liquid, a flask may be set upon wire gauze on a tripod and secured with an iron ring or clamp on a stand. The flame is extinguished by turning off the gas at the source.

Safety Procedures Related to Animals

Animals to be used for **dissections** should be obtained from a company that provides animals for this purpose. Road kill or decaying animals that a student brings in should not be used. It is possible that such an animal may have a pathogen or a virus, such as rabies, which can be transmitted via the saliva of even a dead animal. Students should use gloves and should not participate if they have open sores or moral objections to dissections. It is generally accepted that biological experiments may be performed on lower-order life forms and invertebrates, but not on mammalian vertebrates and birds. No animals should be harmed physiologically. Experimental animals should be kept, cared for, and handled in a safe manner and with compassion. Pathogenic (anything able to cause a disease) substances should not be used in lab experiments.

Lab Notebooks

A **lab notebook** is a record of all pre-lab work and lab work. It differs from a lab report, which is prepared after lab work is completed. A lab notebook is a formal record of lab preparations and what was done. **Observational recordings** should not be altered, erased, or whited-out to make corrections. Drawing a single line through an entry is sufficient to make changes. Pages should be numbered and should not be torn out. Entries should be made neatly, but don't necessarily have to be complete sentences. **Entries** should provide detailed information and be recorded in such a way that another person could use them to replicate the experiment. **Quantitative data** may be recorded in tabular form, and may include calculations made during an experiment. Lab book entries can also include references and research performed before the experiment. Entries may also consist of information about a lab experiment, including the objective or purpose, the procedures, data collected, and the results.

Lab Reports

A **lab report** is an item developed after an experiment that is intended to present the results of a lab experiment. Generally, it should be prepared using a word processor, not hand-written or recorded in a notebook. A lab report should be formally presented. It is intended to persuade others to accept or reject a hypothesis. It should include a brief but descriptive **title** and an **abstract**. The abstract is a summary of the report. It should include a purpose that states the problem that was explored or the question that was answered. It should also include a **hypothesis** that describes the anticipated results of the experiment. The experiment should include a **control** and one **variable** to ensure that the results can be interpreted correctly. Observations and results can be presented using written narratives, tables, graphs, and illustrations. The report should also include a **summation** or **conclusion** explaining whether the results supported the hypothesis.

Types of Laboratory Glassware

Two types of flasks are Erlenmeyer flasks and volumetric flasks. **Volumetric flasks** are used to accurately prepare a specific volume and concentration of a solution. **Erlenmeyer flasks** can be used for mixing, transporting, and reacting, but are not appropriate for accurate measurements.

A **pipette** can be used to accurately measure small amounts of liquid. Liquid is drawn into the pipette through a bulb. The liquid measurement is read at the **meniscus**. There are also plastic disposable pipettes. A **repipette** is a hand-operated pump that dispenses solutions.

Beakers can be used to measure mass or dissolve a solvent into a solute. They do not measure volume as accurately as a volumetric flask, pipette, graduated cylinder, or burette.

Graduated cylinders are used for precise measurements and are considered more accurate than Erlenmeyer flasks or beakers. To read a graduated cylinder, it should be placed on a flat surface and read at eye level. The surface of a liquid in a graduated cylinder forms a lens-shaped curve. The measurement should be taken from the bottom of the curve. A ring may be placed at the top of tall, narrow cylinders to help avoid breakage if they are tipped over.

A **burette**, or buret, is a piece of lab glassware used to accurately dispense liquid. It looks similar to a narrow graduated cylinder, but it includes a stopcock and tip. It may be filled with a funnel or pipette.

Microscopes

There are different kinds of microscopes, but **optical** or **light microscopes** are the most commonly used in lab settings. Light and lenses are used to magnify and view samples. A specimen or sample is placed on a slide, and the slide is placed on a stage with a hole in it. Light passes through the hole and illuminates the sample. The sample is magnified by lenses and viewed through the eyepiece. A simple microscope has one lens, while a typical compound microscope has three lenses. The light source can be room light redirected by a mirror, or the microscope can have its own independent light source that passes through a condenser. In this case, there are diaphragms and filters to allow light intensity to be controlled. Optical microscopes also have coarse and fine adjustment knobs.

Other types of microscopes include **digital microscopes**, which use a camera and a monitor to allow viewing of the sample. **Scanning electron microscopes (SEMs)** provide greater detail in terms of a sample's surface topography and can produce magnifications much greater than those possible with optical microscopes. The technology of an SEM is quite different from an optical microscope in that it does not rely on lenses to magnify objects, but uses samples placed in a chamber. In one type of SEM, a beam of electrons from an electron gun scans and actually interacts with the sample to produce an image.

Wet mount slides designed for use with a light microscope typically require a thin portion of the specimen to be placed on a standard glass slide. A drop of water is added, and a cover slip or cover glass is placed on top. Air bubbles and fingerprints can make viewing difficult. Placing the cover slip at a 45-degree angle and allowing it to drop into place can help avoid the problem of air bubbles. A **cover slip** should always be used when viewing wet mount slides. The viewer should start with the objective in its lowest position and then fine-focus. The microscope should be carried with two hands and stored with the low-power objective in the down position. **Lenses** should be cleaned with lens paper only. A **graticule slide** is marked with a grid line, and is useful for counting or estimating a quantity.

Balances

Balances such as triple-beam balances, spring balances, and electronic balances measure mass and force. An **electronic balance** is the most accurate, followed by a **triple-beam balance** and then a **spring balance**. One part of a **triple-beam balance** is the plate, which is where the item to be weighed is placed. There are also three beams, which have hash marks indicating amounts and which hold the weights that rest in the notches. The front beam measures weights between 0 and 10 grams, the middle beam measures weights in 100-gram increments, and the far beam measures weights in 10-gram increments. The sum of the weight of each beam is the total weight of the object. A triple beam balance also includes a set screw to calibrate the equipment, as well as a mark indicating that the object and counterweights are in balance.

Chromatography

Chromatography refers to a set of laboratory techniques used to separate or analyze **mixtures**. Mixtures are dissolved in their mobile phases. In the stationary or bonded phase, the desired component is separated from other molecules in the mixture. In chromatography, the analyte is the substance to be separated. **Preparative chromatography** refers to the type of chromatography that involves purifying a substance for further use rather than further analysis. **Analytical chromatography** involves analyzing the isolated substance. Other types of chromatography include column, planar, paper, thin layer, displacement, supercritical fluid, affinity, ion exchange, and size exclusion chromatography. Reversed phase, two-dimensional, simulated moving bed, pyrolysis, fast protein, counter current, and chiral are also types of chromatography. **Gas**

chromatography refers to the separation technique in which the mobile phase of a substance is in gas form.

Review Video: Paper Chromatography
Visit mometrix.com/academy and enter code: 543963

Reagents and Reactants

A **reagent** or **reactant** is a chemical agent for use in chemical reactions. When preparing for a lab, it should be confirmed that glassware and other equipment have been cleaned and/or sterilized. There should be enough materials, reagents, or other solutions needed for the lab for every group of students completing the experiment. Distilled water should be used instead of tap water when performing lab experiments because distilled water has most of its impurities removed. Other needed apparatus such as funnels, filter paper, balances, Bunsen burners, ring stands, and/or microscopes should also be set up. After the lab, it should be confirmed that sinks, workstations, and any equipment used have been cleaned. If chemicals or specimens need to be kept at a certain temperature by refrigerating them or using another storage method, the temperature should be checked periodically to ensure the sample does not spoil.

Diluting Acids

When preparing a solution of **dilute acid**, always add the concentrated acid solution to water, not water to concentrated acid. Start by adding approximately $\frac{2}{3}$ of the total volume of water to the graduated cylinder or volumetric flask. Next, add the concentrated acid to the water. Add additional water to the diluted acid to bring the solution to the final desired volume.

Cleaning After Acid Spills

In the event of an **acid spill**, any clothes that have come into contact with the acid should be removed and any skin contacted with acid must be rinsed with clean water. To the extent a window can be opened or a fume hood can be turned on, do so. Do not try to force air circulation, such as by adding a fan, as acid fumes can be harmful if spread.

Next, pour one of the following over the spill area: sodium bicarbonate, baking soda, soda ash, or cat litter. Start from the outside of the spill and then move towards the center, in order to prevent splashing. When the clumps have thoroughly dried, sweep up the clumps and dispose of them as chemical waste.

Centrifuges

A centrifuge is used to separate the components of a heterogeneous mixture (consisting of two or more compounds) by spinning it. The solid precipitate settles in the bottom of the container, and the liquid component of the solution, called the **centrifugate**, is at the top. A well-known application of this process is using a centrifuge to separate blood cells and plasma. The heavier cells settle on the bottom of the test tube, and the lighter plasma stays on top. Another example is using a salad spinner to help dry lettuce.

Electrophoresis, Calorimetry, and Titration

- **Electrophoresis** is the separation of molecules based on electrical charge. This is possible because particles dispersed in a fluid usually carry electric charges on their surfaces. Molecules are pulled through the fluid toward the positive end if the molecules have a negative charge and are pulled through the fluid toward the negative end if the molecules have a positive charge.
- **Calorimetry** is used to determine the heat released or absorbed in a chemical reaction.
- **Titration** helps determine the precise endpoint of a reaction. With this information, the precise quantity of reactant in the titration flask can be determined. A burette is used to deliver the second reactant to the flask and an indicator or pH meter is used to detect the endpoint of the reaction.

Field Studies and Research Projects

Field studies may facilitate scientific inquiry in a manner similar to indoor lab experiments. Field studies can be interdisciplinary in nature and can help students learn and apply scientific concepts and processes. **Research projects** can be conducted in any number of locations, including school campuses, local parks, national parks, beaches, or mountains. Students can practice the general techniques of observation, data collection, collaborative planning, and analysis of experiments. Field studies give students the chance to learn through hands-on applications of scientific processes, such as map making in geography, observation of stratification in geology, observation of life cycles of plants and animals, and analysis of water quality.

Students should watch out for obvious outdoor **hazards**. These include poisonous flora and fauna such as poison ivy, poison oak, and sumac. Depending on the region of the United States in which the field study is being conducted, hazards may also include rattlesnakes and black widow or brown recluse spiders. Students should also be made aware of potentially hazardous situations specific to **geographic locales** and the possibility of coming into contact with **pathogens**.

Field studies allow for great flexibility in the use of traditional and technological methods for **making observations** and **collecting data**. For example, a nature study could consist of a simple survey of bird species within a given area. Information could be recorded using still photography or a video camera. This type of activity gives students the chance to use technologies other than computers. Computers could still be used to create a slide show of transferred images or a digital lab report. If a quantitative study of birds was being performed, the simple technique of using a pencil and paper to tabulate the number of birds counted in the field could also be used. Other techniques used during field studies could include collecting specimens for lab study, observing coastal ecosystems and tides, and collecting weather data such as temperature, precipitation amounts, and air pressure in a particular locale.

Scientific Concepts Related to Biology

Chemical Nature of Biology

All organisms are made up of matter and display the typical physical and chemical properties of matter. Every cell of an organism is composed of molecules, atoms, and ions. **Chemistry** is needed to explain the structure and function of all cellular processes at the molecular level. **Organic chemistry** involves many large and complex molecules including biochemical compounds like carbohydrates, lipids, proteins, and nucleic acids. Chemical reactions occur in the daily function of organisms even at the cellular level. Chemical reactions that are important for life include oxidation-reduction, dehydration synthesis, hydrolysis, phosphorylation, and acid-base reactions.

Use of Mathematics in Biology

Mathematics is becoming increasingly prevalent in modern biology, especially with the use of computers for statistical programs. Mathematics is used in the **studies of populations**. For example, biologists study human population growth, bacteria growth, and virus growth. Populations of organisms in feeding relationships such as predator and prey are studied. Mathematics is used in classical genetics. For example, biologists use probability theory to predict offspring in **genetic crosses**. Mathematics, with the help of computer science, is used extensively in bioinformatics to analyze large amounts of biological information. For example, biological data are extracted and analyzed using sophisticated computer programing. Mathematics is also used in studies of epidemics. For example, studies concerning the spread of the flu and acquired immune deficiency syndrome (AIDS) have been performed.

Physical Laws and Principles Governing Biological Systems

Biological systems are governed by the same physical laws and principles that govern the rest of the universe. For example, biological systems must obey the laws of thermodynamics. These laws govern energy and the transformations of energy. The first law of thermodynamics is the law of **conservation of energy**, which states that energy is neither created nor destroyed but can change forms. The energy needed for life on Earth comes from the Sun. Sunlight reaches the Earth and is transformed by green plants and cyanobacteria (producers) during photosynthesis into the chemical bonds of ATP molecules, which can be used by these organisms for energy. Consumers eat the producers or other consumers in order to obtain energy. The second law of thermodynamics states that systems tend toward more disorder or randomness, also known as **entropy**. This is evident in the fact that organisms must continually acquire or transfer energy to sustain life and, as such, the energy is dispersed through the whole biosphere. This diffusion of energy isn't perfectly efficient and much of the energy becomes heat and is essentially unusable.

Cell Theory

Cell theory states that all living things are composed of cells, which are the basic unit of structure and function in living things, and that cells come from preexisting cells. Cells were first observed in 1655 by Robert Hooke when he was studying thin slices of a piece of cork under his primitive microscope. Because the cork cells were dead, Hooke actually only observed the cell walls of the cork cells. Hooke was the first to use the word "cell," which comes from the Latin word *cellula*, which means small compartment. Hooke documented his observations with sketches and published his work in his book commonly called *Micrographia.*

Germ Theory of Disease

The **germ theory of disease** states that most infectious diseases are caused by germs or disease-causing microbes or pathogens. The germ theory is the foundation of microbiology and modern medicine. Pasteur studied the fermentation of wine and the spoiling of milk. He discovered that yeast caused the fermentation of wine and bacteria caused the spoiling of milk. He developed the process of pasteurization of milk that killed the harmful microbes without ruining the taste of the milk. Then he studied diseases in silkworms and was able to determine that the causes of those diseases were protozoa and bacteria. Pasteur also thought that microbes in hospitals came from preexisting microbes instead of **spontaneous generation**. He disproved spontaneous generation with his work with bacteria and broth. He discovered that weakened microbes could be used in **vaccines** or **immunizations** to prevent or protect against the diseases caused by those microbes. Pasteur discovered viruses in his work, developing the rabies vaccine and treatments for those already infected with the rabies virus.

Mendel's Contributions to Genetics

Johann Gregor Mendel is known as the **father of genetics**. Mendel was an Austrian monk who performed thousands of experiments involving the breeding of the common pea plant in the monastery garden. Mendel kept detailed records including seed color, pod color, seed type, flower color, and plant height for eight years and published his work in 1865. Unfortunately, his work was largely ignored until the early 1900s. Mendel's work showed that genes come in pairs and that dominant and recessive traits are inherited independently of each other. His work established the law of segregation, the law of independent assortment, and the law of dominance.

Darwin's Contributions to Theory of Evolution

Charles Darwin's **theory of evolution** by natural selection is the unifying concept in biology today. From 1831 to 1836, Darwin traveled as a naturalist on a five-year voyage on the *H.M.S. Beagle* around the tip of South America and to the Galápagos Islands. He studied finches, took copious amounts of meticulous notes, and collected thousands of plant and animal specimens. He collected 13 species of finches, each with a unique bill for a distinct food source These similarities between the finches led him to believe that the finches shared a common ancestor. The similarities and differences of fossils of extinct rodents and modern mammal fossils led him to believe that the mammals had changed over time. Darwin believed that these changes were the result of random genetic changes called **mutations**. He believed that mutations could be beneficial and eventually result in a different organism over time. In 1859, in his first book, *On the Origin of Species*, Darwin coined the term "**natural selection**" and proposed that it was the means by which adaptations would arise over time. He said that it is the mechanism of evolution. Because variety exists among individuals of a species, he stated that those individuals must compete for the same limited resources. Some would die, and others would survive. According to Darwin, evolution is a slow, gradual process. In 1871, Darwin published his second book, *Descent of Man, and Selection in Relation to Sex*, in which he discussed the evolution of man.

Contribution to Genetics by Alfred Hershey and Martha Chase

Alfred Hershey and Martha Chase did a series of experiments in 1952 known as the **Hershey-Chase experiments**. These experiments showed that deoxyribonucleic acid (DNA), not protein, is the genetic material that transfers information for inheritance. The Hershey-Chase experiments used a bacteriophage, a virus that infects bacteria, to infect the bacteria *Escherichia coli.* The bacteriophage T2 is basically a small piece of DNA enclosed in a protein coating. The DNA contains phosphorus, and the protein coating contains sulfur. In the first set of experiments, the T2 was marked with radioactive phosphorus-32. In the second set of experiments, the T2 was marked with radioactive sulfur-35. For both sets of experiments, after the *E. coli* was infected by the T2, the *E. coli* was isolated using a centrifuge. In the first set of experiments, the radioactive isotope (P-32) was found in the *E. coli*, showing that the genetic information was transferred by the DNA. In the second set of experiments, the radioactive isotope (S-35) was not found in the *E. coli*, showing that the genetic information was not transferred by the protein as was previously thought. Hershey and Chase conducted further experiments allowing the bacteria from the first set of experiments to reproduce, and the offspring was also found to contain the radioactive isotope (P-32) further confirming that the DNA transferred the genetic material.

Contributions to the Knowledge of DNA

The three-dimensional double-helix structure of the DNA molecule was formulated by James Watson and Francis Crick in 1953. But the actual discovery of DNA took place in 1869 when Friedrich Miescher discovered DNA, which he called "nuclein" in the nuclei of human white blood cells while attempting to isolate proteins. Years later in 1919, Phoebus Levene identified the components of a nucleotide. Then in 1950, Erwin Chargaff published his discovery that DNA varies among species and states what is now known as **Chargaff's rule**: Adenine always combines with thymine, and cytosine always combines with guanine. In 1951, Rosalind Franklin studied the molecular structure of DNA using x-rays. Her work laid the foundation for the work that Watson and Crick did in 1953, in which they discovered the three-dimensional double-helix structure of DNA. Watson and Crick showed that the complementary bases are joined by hydrogen bonds. Franklin also studied the structure of RNA and discovered that RNA is a single-strand helix structure, not a double strand like DNA.

Population Models

Ecologists use population models to study the populations in an ecosystem and their interactions of populations with the environment. **Population models** are mathematical models that are designed to study population dynamics. Ecologists can model the growth of a population. For example, models can be designed to describe increases, decreases, or fluctuations in the size of populations due to births, deaths, and migrations. Ecologists can model the interactions of populations with other populations. For example, models of the interactions between predator and prey describe the fluctuating cycles associated with these relationships. Models can also include other factors such as diseases and limiting resources.

Ethical Concerns of Embryonic Stem Cells for Research

Research involving the use of embryonic stem cells offers hope for genetics-related health issues. However, ethical issues are seriously debated. New therapies could be developed using embryonic stem cells that would greatly alleviate suffering for many people. However, that benefit comes at the cost of human embryos. Proponents of embryonic stem cell research argue that an early embryo is not yet a person because the embryo cannot survive without being implanted in the uterus. Some believe that the embryo should have no moral status and that fertilized eggs should be treated as the property of the parents who should have the right to donate that property to research. Opponents of embryonic stem cell research argue that the embryo is a human life at fertilization and should have full moral status at fertilization, and that a human embryo is a human being. Opponents argue that judgments determining when an embryo is viable or when an embryo is fully human cannot be made. Some opponents of stem cell research do not believe that the fertilized egg is a human being, but they still argue that by removing the stem cells from the early embryo, the embryo is prevented from becoming a human being. They argue that embryonic stem cell research destroys potential life.

Ethical and Societal Concerns Regarding Genetically Modified Food

Genetically modified (GM) foods are transgenic crops that have had their genes altered by technology. For example, herbicide-tolerant soybeans and insect-resistant corn have been grown for years in the United States. Several issues have been raised concerning GM foods. Some people do not want to go against nature. Even scientists may feel that because the genes in organisms have evolved over millions of years that man should not interfere. Others would argue that man has been selectively breeding plants and animals for hundreds of years, and genetic modification is just an extension of that concept. Scientists are concerned about introducing new allergens into the food supply. For example, if a gene from a peanut plant is introduced into a soybean plant, there may be a potential for allergic reactions. Proteins from microorganisms may have never been tested as allergens. Many are concerned that the genetic modifications will not be contained. Pollen from fields of genetically modified crops may be carried by insects or wind to other fields. In some cases, traits such as herbicide resistance might pass from the cultivated plants to the wild populations of those plants. Insect-resistant plants may harm insects other than those that were being targeted.

For example, studies show that pollinators such as the monarch butterfly may be harmed from GM corn.

Ethical Concerns Regarding Human Cloning and Animal Cloning

Many issues are raised with the topic of human cloning and animal cloning. Disagreements arise over who, if any, should be allowed to produce human clones. Many are concerned about how clones would integrate into families and societies. Some believe that human cloning for procreation purposes should be regulated based on motivation. For example, individuals interested in raising a genetically-related child should be granted approval, but those seeking immortality or viewing cloning as a novelty should be denied. Many believe that mandatory counseling and a waiting period should be enforced. Others argue that individuals do not have a right to a genetically-related child, that cloning is not safe, and that cloning is not medically necessary. Proponents argue that cloning is needed to generate tissues and whole organs that eliminate the need for immunosuppressive drugs. Cloned tissues and organs could be used to counter the effects of aging. Others fear that this will lead to the generation of humans solely for the purpose of harvesting tissues and organs. Animals are being cloned in laboratories and in livestock production. Animal rights activists are opposed to the cloning of animals and argue that many cloned animals suffer from defects before they die. Some believe that animals have moral rights and should be treated with the same ethical consideration given to humans.

Societal Concerns About Genetic Testing

Society has not fully embraced genetic testing. Many people do not consider genetic testing to be a medical test and many feel pressure from family members who do not want the family genes revealed. Some do not want to know of potential health problems they may face later in life. Many are concerned about the psychological impact and stigma associated with carrying gene mutations. Others fear genetic discrimination from employers such as not being hired, losing a job, or being denied promotions. Some people fear being denied services from health insurers, while others fear being denied educational opportunities. However, the Genetic Information Nondiscrimination Act of 2008 protects Americans from discrimination due to differences in their DNA.

Concerns about privacy and confidentiality in regard to genetic testing raise questions that have yet to be answered. For example, who owns an individual's genetic information and who has access to that information? Should courts and schools have access to that information? Genetic testing also raises philosophical issues. Do genes determine behavior? If so, then are people responsible for their behavior?

Genetic Engineering

Genetic engineering is putting DNA from one species into another species. DNA from a species with desirable traits is spliced into the chromosomes in cells of other species. Through mitosis, those transgenic cells produce other similar cells, which are cultured to produce new organisms. Food produced by using these transgenic organisms is called GM (genetically modified) food. There is controversy over the safety of GM foods.

Genetic engineering is much faster than the older process—artificial selection—used to make better agricultural plants and animals. In agriculture, desirable traits include better resistance to pests and disease, quicker growth, and development of more of the edible parts. Genetic engineering may also produce plants that need less investment of water or fertilizer, are more resistant to drought and poor soil conditions, and spoil less when stored or transported.

Scientific Inquiry and Reasoning

Scientific Inquiry

The concept of **scientific inquiry** refers to the idea of how one thinks and asks questions in a logical way to gain trustworthy information. The underlying motivation of science is to try to understand the natural world. Much of human thought is based on assumptions about how things work that may or may not be true. The goal of scientific inquiry is to test those assumptions to gain a greater understanding of the world with good questions and objective tests, and then re-use what was learned to ask better questions. The more we understand about the natural world, the better the questions we can ask, and that is the general idea behind scientific inquiry. The applied practice of scientific inquiry is to ask questions in a systematic method, called the scientific method.

Scientific Knowledge

Scientific knowledge refers to any topic that is studied **empirically**, meaning that it is based on observation of a **phenomenon** in an objective way. The body of **scientific knowledge** is often broken down into several domains including biology, ecology, Earth science, space science, physics, and chemistry. These each have further subdomains and are overlapping in many ways. For instance, ecology is the study of ecosystems, which are made up of biological factors and geological factors, so it contains elements of both biology and Earth science. Each of these domains is subject to the concepts of scientific inquiry, such as the scientific method, scientific facts, hypotheses, and scientific laws.

Important Terminology

- A **phenomenon** is an event or effect that is observed.
- A **scientific fact** is considered an objective and verifiable observation. Usually, a fact can be repeated or demonstrated to others.
- A **scientific theory** is a proposition explaining why or how something happens and is built on scientific facts and laws. Scientific theories can be tested, but are not fully proven. If new evidence is found that disproves the theory, it is no longer considered true.
- A **hypothesis** is an educated guess that is not yet proven. It is used to predict the outcome of an experiment in an attempt to solve a problem or answer a question.
- A **law** is an explanation of events that always leads to the same outcome. It is a fact that an object falls. The law of gravity explains why an object falls. The theory of relativity, although generally accepted, has been neither proven nor disproved.
- A **model** is used to explain something on a smaller scale or in simpler terms to provide an example. It is a representation of an idea that can be used to explain events or applied to new situations to predict outcomes or determine results.

History of Scientific Knowledge

When one examines the history of **scientific knowledge**, it is clear that it is constantly **evolving**. The body of facts, models, theories, and laws grows and changes over time. In other words, one scientific discovery leads to the next. Some advances in science and technology have important and long-lasting effects on science and society. Some discoveries were so alien to the accepted beliefs of the time that not only were they rejected as wrong, but were also considered outright blasphemy. Today, however, many beliefs once considered incorrect have become an ingrained part of scientific knowledge, and have also been the basis of new advances. Examples of advances include: Copernicus's heliocentric view of the universe, Newton's laws of motion and planetary orbits, relativity, geologic time scale, plate tectonics, atomic theory, nuclear physics, biological evolution, germ theory, industrial revolution, molecular biology, information and communication, quantum theory, galactic universe, and medical and health technology.

Scientific Inquiry and Scientific Method

Scientists use a number of generally accepted techniques collectively known as the **scientific method**. The scientific method generally involves carrying out the following steps:

- Identifying a problem or posing a question
- Formulating a hypothesis or an educated guess
- Conducting experiments or tests that will provide a basis to solve the problem or answer the question
- Observing the results of the test
- Drawing conclusions

An important part of the scientific method is using acceptable experimental techniques. Objectivity is also important if valid results are to be obtained. Another important part of the scientific method is peer review. It is essential that experiments be performed and data be recorded in such a way that experiments can be reproduced to verify results. Historically, the scientific method has been taught with a more linear approach, but it is important to recognize that the scientific method should be a cyclical or **recursive process**. This means that as hypotheses are tested and more is learned, the questions should continue to change to reflect the changing body of knowledge. One cycle of experimentation is not enough.

Review Video: The Scientific Method
Visit mometrix.com/academy and enter code: 191386

Metric and International System of Units

The **metric system** is the accepted standard of measurement in the scientific community. The **International System of Units (SI)** is a set of measurements (including the metric system) that is almost globally accepted. The United States, Liberia, and Myanmar have not accepted this system. **Standardization** is important because it allows the results of experiments to be compared and reproduced without the need to laboriously convert measurements. The SI is based partially on the **meter-kilogram-second (MKS) system** rather than the **centimeter-gram-second (CGS) system**. The MKS system considers meters, kilograms, and seconds to be the basic units of measurement, while the CGS system considers centimeters, grams, and seconds to be the basic units of measurement. Under the MKS system, the length of an object would be expressed as 1 meter instead of 100 centimeters, which is how it would be described under the CGS system.

Review Video: Metric System Conversions
Visit mometrix.com/academy and enter code: 163709

Basic Units of Measurement

Using the **metric system** is generally accepted as the preferred method for taking measurements. Having a **universal standard** allows individuals to interpret measurements more easily, regardless of where they are located. The basic units of measurement are: the **meter**, which measures length; the **liter**, which measures volume; and the **gram**, which measures mass. The metric system starts with a base unit and increases or decreases in units of 10. The prefix and the base unit combined are used to indicate an amount. For example, deka- is 10 times the base unit. A dekameter is 10 meters; a dekaliter is 10 liters; and a dekagram is 10 grams. The prefix hecto- refers to 100 times the base amount; kilo- is 1,000 times the base amount. The prefixes that indicate a fraction of the base unit are deci-, which is $\frac{1}{10}$ of the base unit; centi-, which is $\frac{1}{100}$ of the base unit; and milli-, which is $\frac{1}{1,000}$ of the base unit.

Common Prefixes

The prefixes for multiples are as follows:

Deka	(da)	**10^1** (deka is the American spelling, but deca is also used)
Hecto	(h)	10^2
Kilo	(k)	10^3
Mega	(M)	10^6
Giga	(G)	10^9
Tera	(T)	10^{12}

The prefixes for subdivisions are as follows:

Deci	(d)	**10^{-1}**
Centi	(c)	10^{-2}
Milli	(m)	10^{-3}
Micro	(μ)	10^{-6}
Nano	(n)	10^{-9}
Pico	(p)	10^{-12}

The rule of thumb is that prefixes greater than 10^3 are capitalized when abbreviating. Abbreviations do not need a period after them. A decimeter (dm) is a tenth of a meter, a deciliter (dL) is a tenth of a liter, and a decigram (dg) is a tenth of a gram. Pluralization is understood. For example, when referring to 5 mL of water, no "s" needs to be added to the abbreviation.

Basic SI Units of Measurement

SI uses **second(s)** to measure time. Fractions of seconds are usually measured in metric terms using prefixes such as millisecond ($\frac{1}{1,000}$ of a second) or nanosecond ($\frac{1}{1,000,000,000}$ of a second). Increments of time larger than a second are measured in **minutes** and **hours**, which are multiples of 60 and 24. An example of this is a swimmer's time in the 800-meter freestyle being described as 7:32.67, meaning 7 minutes, 32 seconds, and 67 one-hundredths of a second. One second is equal to $\frac{1}{60}$ of a minute, $\frac{1}{3,600}$ of an hour, and $\frac{1}{86,400}$ of a day. Other SI base units are the **ampere** (A) (used to measure electric current), the **kelvin** (K) (used to measure thermodynamic temperature), the **candela** (cd) (used to measure luminous intensity), and the **mole** (mol) (used to measure the amount of a substance at a molecular level). **Meter** (m) is used to measure length and **kilogram** (kg) is used to measure mass.

Significant Figures

The mathematical concept of **significant figures** or **significant digits** is often used to determine the accuracy of measurements or the level of confidence one has in a specific measurement. The significant figures of a measurement include all the digits known with certainty plus one estimated or uncertain digit. There are a number of rules for determining which digits are considered "important" or "interesting." They are:

- All non-zero digits are *significant.*
- Zeros between digits are *significant.*
- Leading and trailing zeros are *not significant* unless they appear to the right of the non-zero digits in a decimal.

For example, in 0.01230, the significant digits are 1230, and this number would be said to be accurate to the hundred-thousandths place. The zero indicates that the amount has actually been measured as 0. Other zeros are considered placeholders and are not important. A decimal point may be placed after zeros to indicate their importance (in "100." for example).

Graphs and Charts

Graphs and charts are effective ways to present scientific data such as observations, statistical analyses, and comparisons between dependent variables and independent variables. On a line chart, the **independent variable** (the one that is being manipulated for the experiment) is represented on the horizontal axis (the x-axis). Any **dependent variables** (the ones that may change as the independent variable changes) are represented on the y-axis. An **XY** or **scatter plot** is often used to plot many points. A "best fit" line is drawn, which allows outliers to be identified more easily. Charts and their axes should have titles. The x and y interval units should be evenly spaced and labeled. Other types of charts are **bar charts** and **histograms**, which can be used to compare differences between the data collected for two variables. A **pie chart** can graphically show the relation of parts to a whole.

Review Video: Identifying Variables
Visit mometrix.com/academy and enter code: 627181

Review Video: Data Interpretation of Graphs
Visit mometrix.com/academy and enter code: 200439

Data Presentation

Data collected during a science lab can be organized and **presented** in any number of ways. While **straight narrative** is a suitable method for presenting some lab results, it is not a suitable way to present numbers and quantitative measurements. These types of observations can often be better presented with **tables** and **graphs**. Data that is presented in tables and organized in rows and columns may also be used to make graphs quite easily. Other methods of presenting data include illustrations, photographs, video, and even audio formats. In a **formal report**, tables and figures are labeled and referred to by their labels. For example, a picture of a bubbly solution might be labeled Figure 1, Bubbly Solution. It would be referred to in the text in the following way: "The reaction created bubbles 10 mm in size, as shown in Figure 1, Bubbly Solution." Graphs are also labeled as figures. Tables are labeled in a different way. Examples include: Table 1, Results of Statistical Analysis, or Table 2, Data from Lab 2.

Statistical Precision and Errors

Errors that occur during an experiment can be classified into two categories: random errors and systematic errors. **Random errors** can result in collected data that is wildly different from the rest of the data, or they may result in data that is indistinguishable from the rest. Random errors are not consistent across the data set. In large data sets, random errors may contribute to the variability of data, but they will not affect the average. Random errors are sometimes referred to as noise. They may be caused by a student's inability to take the same measurement in exactly the same way or by outside factors that are not considered variables, but influence the data. A **systematic error** will show up consistently across a sample or data set, and may be the result of a flaw in the experimental design. This type of error affects the average, and is also known as bias.

Scientific Notation

Scientific notation is used because values in science can be very large or very small, which makes them unwieldy. A number in **decimal notation** is 93,000,000. In **scientific notation**, it is 9.3×10^7. The first number, 9.3, is the **coefficient**. It is always greater than or equal to 1 and less than 10. This number is followed by a multiplication sign. The base is always 10 in scientific notation. If the number is greater than ten, the exponent is positive. If the number is between zero and one, the exponent is negative. The first digit of the number is followed by a decimal point and then the rest of the number. In this case, the number is 9.3, and the decimal point was moved seven places to the right from the end of the number to get 93,000,000. The number of places moved, seven, is the exponent.

Statistical Terminology

- **Mean**—The average, found by taking the sum of a set of numbers and dividing by the number of numbers in the set.
- **Median**—The middle number in a set of numbers sorted from least to greatest. If the set has an even number of entries, the median is the average of the two in the middle.
- **Mode**—The value that appears most frequently in a data set. There may be more than one mode. If no value appears more than once, there is no mode.
- **Range**—The difference between the highest and lowest numbers in a data set.
- **Standard deviation**—Measures the dispersion of a data set, or how far from the mean a single data point is likely to be.
- **Regression analysis**—A method of analyzing sets of data and sets of variables. It involves studying how the typical value of the dependent variable changes when any one of the independent variables is varied and the other independent variables remain fixed.

Review Video: Mean, Median, and Mode
Visit mometrix.com/academy and enter code: 286207

Review Video: Standard Deviation
Visit mometrix.com/academy and enter code: 419469

Chapter Quiz

Ready to see how well you retained what you just read? Scan the QR code to go directly to the chapter quiz interface for this study guide. If you're using a computer, simply visit the online resources page at **mometrix.com/resources719/ssreglivingenv** and click the Chapter Quizzes link.

Cells

Chemical Structures and Properties of Biologically Important Molecules

Chemical Bonding Properties of Carbon

Carbon is considered to be the central atom of organic compounds. Carbon atoms each have four valence electrons and require four more electrons to have a stable outer shell. Due to the repulsion between the valence electrons, the bond sites are all equidistant from each other. This enables carbon to form longs chains and rings. Carbon atoms can form four single covalent bonds with other atoms. For example, methane (CH_4) consists of one carbon atom singly bonded to four separate hydrogen atoms. Carbon atoms can also form double or triple covalent bonds. For example, an oxygen atom can form a double bond with a carbon atom, and a nitrogen atom can form a triple bond with a carbon atom.

Organic and Inorganic Molecules

Organic molecules contain carbon and hydrogen. Because carbon can form four covalent bonds, organic molecules can be very complex structures. Organic molecules can have carbon backbones that form long chains, branched chains, or even rings. Organic compounds tend to be less soluble in water than inorganic compounds. Organic compounds are often classified as either natural (found in plants and animals) or as synthetic (made via laboratory or industrial processes). **Inorganic molecules** generally do not contain carbon-carbon or carbon-hydrogen bonds, but there are some exceptions. Inorganic compounds include salts and metals. Specific examples of inorganic molecules include sodium chloride, oxygen, and carbon dioxide.

Covalent Bonds

Chemical bonds are the attractive forces that bind atoms together to form molecules. Chemical bonds include covalent bonds, ionic bonds, and metallic bonds. **Covalent bonds** are formed from the sharing of electron pairs between two atoms in a molecule. In organic molecules, carbon atoms form single, double, or triple covalent bonds. Organic compounds including proteins, carbohydrates, lipids, and nucleic acids are molecular compounds formed by covalent bonds.

Review Video: Covalent Bonds
Visit mometrix.com/academy and enter code: 482899

Hydrogen Bonds

Intermolecular forces are the attractive forces between molecules. Intermolecular forces include hydrogen bonds, London or dispersion forces, and dipole-dipole forces. **Hydrogen bonds** are the attractive forces between molecules containing hydrogen atoms covalently bonded to oxygen, fluorine, or nitrogen. Hydrogen bonds bind the two strands of a DNA molecule to each other. Two hydrogen bonds join each adenosine and thymine, and three hydrogen bonds join each cytosine and guanine.

ATP

Adenosine triphosphate (ATP) is the energy source for most cellular functions. Each ATP molecule is a nucleotide consisting of a central ribose sugar flanked by a purine base and a chain of three phosphate groups. The purine base is adenine, and when adenine is joined to ribose, an adenosine is formed, explaining the name adenosine triphosphate. If one phosphate is removed from the end of the molecule, adenosine diphosphate (ADP) is formed.

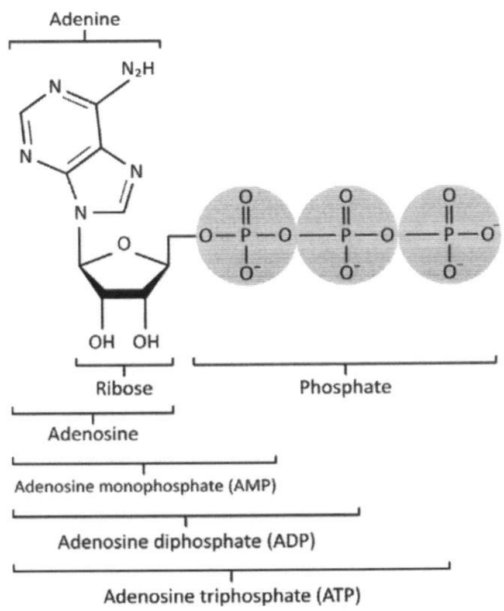

Properties of Water

Water exhibits numerous properties. Water has a high surface tension due to the cohesion between water molecules from the hydrogen bonds between the molecules. The capillary action of water is also due to this cohesion, and the adhesion of water is due to its polarity. Water is an excellent solvent due to its polarity and is considered the universal solvent. Water exists naturally as a solid, liquid, and gas. The density of water decreases as ice freezes and forms crystals in the solid phase. Water is most dense at 4 °C. Water can act as an acid or base in chemical reactions. Pure water is an insulator because it has virtually no ions. Water has a high specific heat capacity due to its low molecular mass and bent molecular shape.

Review Video: Properties of Water
Visit mometrix.com/academy and enter code: 279526

Biological Macromolecules

Macromolecules are large molecules made up of smaller organic molecules. Four classes of macromolecules include carbohydrates, nucleic acids, proteins, and lipids. Carbohydrates, proteins, and nucleic acids are polymers that are formed when the monomers are joined together in a dehydration process. In this dehydration process, the monomers are joined by a covalent bond and a water molecule is released. The monomers in carbohydrates are simple sugars such as glucose, while polysaccharides are polymers of carbohydrates. The monomers in proteins are amino acids. The amino acids form polypeptide chains, which are folded into proteins. The monomers in nucleic acids are nucleotides. Lipids are not actually considered to be polymers. Lipids typically are classified as fats, phospholipids, or steroids.

Review Video: Macromolecules
Visit mometrix.com/academy and enter code: 220156

Biochemical Processes Within an Organism

Concentration Gradients

Concentration gradients, also called diffusion gradients, are differences in the concentration (i.e., the number of molecules of solutes in a solution) between two regions. A gradient can also result from an unequal distribution of ions across a cell membrane. Solutes move along a concentration gradient by random motion from the region of high concentration toward the region of low concentration in a process called diffusion. In other words, **diffusion** is the movement of molecules or ions down a concentration gradient. Diffusion is the method by which oxygen, carbon dioxide, and other nonpolar molecules cross a cell membrane. The steepness of the concentration gradient affects the rate of diffusion. **Passive transport** makes use of concentration gradients as well as electric gradients to move substances across the cell membrane, while **active transport** can move a substance against its concentration gradient.

Laws of Thermodynamics and Gibbs Free Energy

The **first law of thermodynamics** states that energy can neither be created nor destroyed. Energy may change forms, but the energy in a closed system is constant. The **second law of thermodynamics** states that systems tend toward a state of lower energy and greater disorder. This disorder is called **entropy**. According to the second law of thermodynamics, entropy is increasing. **Gibbs free energy** is the energy a system that is available or "free" to be released to perform work at a constant temperature. Organisms must be able to use energy to survive, and biological processes such as the chemical reactions involved in metabolism are governed by these laws.

Anabolic and Catabolic Reactions

Anabolism and catabolism are metabolic processes. **Anabolism** is essentially the synthesis of large molecules from monomers, whereas **catabolism** is the decomposition of large molecules into their component monomers. Anabolism uses energy, whereas catabolism produces energy. Anabolism typically builds and repair tissues, and catabolism typically burns stored food to produce energy. Protein synthesis, which is the polymerization of amino acids to form proteins, is an anabolic reaction. Another anabolic process is the mineralization of bones. An example of a catabolic reaction is hydrolysis, which is the decomposition of polymers into monomers that releases a water molecule and energy. Cellular respiration is a catabolic process in which typically glucose combines with oxygen to release energy in the form of adenosine triphosphate (ATP).

Oxidation-Reduction Reactions

Oxidation-reduction reactions, or redox reactions, involve the transfer of electrons from one substance to another. Reduction occurs in the substance that gains the electrons. Oxidation occurs in the substance that loses the electrons. Cellular respiration and photosynthesis are examples of redox reactions. During cellular respiration, glucose molecules are oxidized and oxygen molecules are reduced. Because electrons lose energy when being transferred to oxygen, the electrons are usually first transferred to the coenzyme NAD^+, which is reduced to NADH. The NADH then releases the energy to oxygen. During photosynthesis, water molecules are split and oxidized and carbon dioxide molecules are reduced. When the water molecules are split, electrons are transferred with the hydrogen ions to the carbon dioxide molecules.

Differences Between Prokaryotic and Eukaryotic Cells

Prokaryotes and Eukaryotes

Sizes and Metabolism

Cells of the domains of Bacteria and Archaea are **prokaryotes**. Bacteria cells and Archaea cells are much smaller than cells of eukaryotes. Prokaryote cells are usually only 1 to 2 micrometers in diameter, but eukaryotic cells are usually at least 10 times and possibly 100 times larger than prokaryotic cells. Eukaryotic cells are usually 10 to 100 micrometers in diameter. Most prokaryotes are unicellular organisms, although some prokaryotes live in colonies. Because of their large surface-area-to-volume ratios, prokaryotes have a very high metabolic rate. **Eukaryotic cells** are much larger than prokaryotic cells. Due to their larger sizes, they have a much smaller surface-area-to-volume ratio and consequently have much lower metabolic rates.

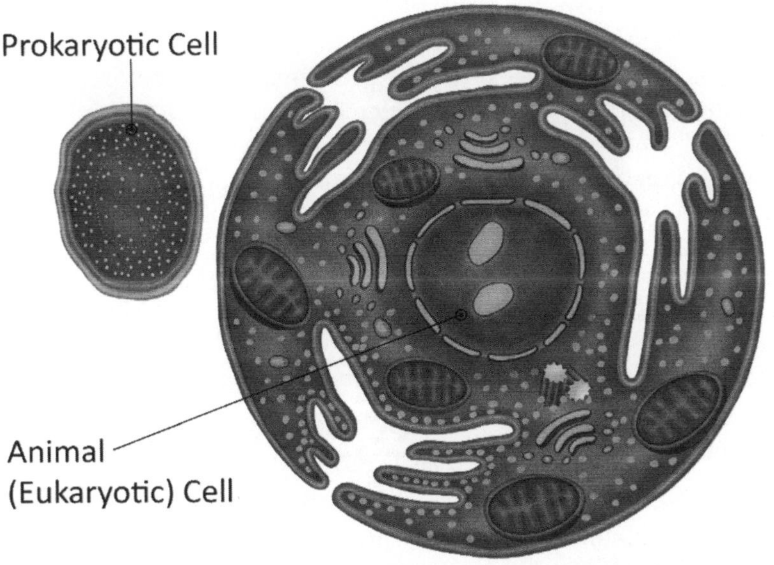

Review Video: Eukaryotic and Prokaryotic Cells
Visit mometrix.com/academy and enter code: 231438

Review Video: Cell Structure
Visit mometrix.com/academy and enter code: 591293

Membrane-Bound Organelles

Prokaryotic cells are much simpler than eukaryotic cells. Prokaryote cells do not have a nucleus due to their small size and their DNA is located in the center of the cell in a region referred to as a **nucleoid**. Eukaryote cells have a **nucleus** bound by a double membrane. Eukaryotic cells typically have hundreds or thousands of additional **membrane-bound organelles** that are independent of the cell membrane. Prokaryotic cells do not have any membrane-bound organelles that are independent of the cell membrane. Once again, this is probably due to the much larger size of the eukaryotic cells. The organelles of eukaryotes give them much higher levels of intracellular division than is possible in prokaryotic cells.

Cell Walls

Not all cells have cell walls, but most prokaryotes have cell walls. The cell walls of organisms from the domain Bacteria differ from the cell walls of the organisms from the domain Archaea. Some eukaryotes, such as some fungi, some algae, and plants, have cell walls that differ from the cell walls of the Bacteria and Archaea domains. The main difference between the cell walls of different domains or kingdoms is the composition of the cell walls. For example, most bacteria have cell walls outside of the plasma membrane that contains the molecule peptidoglycan. **Peptidoglycan** is a large polymer of amino acids and sugars. The peptidoglycan helps maintain the strength of the cell wall. Some of the Archaea cells have cell walls containing the molecule pseudopeptidoglycan, which differs in chemical structure from the peptidoglycan but basically provides the same strength to the cell wall. Some fungi cell walls contain **chitin**. The cell walls of diatoms, a type of yellow algae, contain silica. Plant cell walls contain cellulose, and woody plants are further strengthened by lignin. Some algae also contain lignin. Animal cells do not have cell walls.

Chromosome Structure

Prokaryote cells have DNA arranged in a **circular structure** that should not be referred to as a chromosome. Due to the small size of a prokaryote cell, the DNA material is simply located near the center of the cell in a region called the nucleoid. A prokaryotic cell may also contain tiny rings of DNA called plasmids. Prokaryote cells lack histone proteins, and therefore the DNA is not actually packaged into chromosomes. Prokaryotes reproduce by binary fission, while eukaryotes reproduce by mitosis with the help of **linear chromosomes** and histone proteins. During mitosis, the chromatin is tightly wound on the histone proteins and packaged as a chromosome. The DNA in a eukaryotic cell is located in the membrane-bound nucleus.

Review Video: Chromosomes
Visit mometrix.com/academy and enter code: 132083

Structure and Function of Cells and Organelles

Cells and Organelles of Plant Cells and Animal Cells

Plant cells and animal cells both have a nucleus, cytoplasm, cell membrane, ribosomes, mitochondria, endoplasmic reticulum, Golgi apparatus, and vacuoles. Plant cells have only one or two extremely large vacuoles. Animal cells typically have several small vacuoles. Plant cells have chloroplasts for photosynthesis and use this process to produce their own food, distinguishing plants as **autotrophs**. Animal cells do not have chloroplasts and therefore cannot use photosynthesis to produce their own food. Instead animal cells rely on other sources for food, which classifies them as **heterotrophs**. Animal cells have centrioles, which are used to help organize microtubules and in in cell division, but only some plant cells have centrioles. Additionally, plant cells have a rectangular and more rigid shape due to the cell wall, while animal cells have more of a circular shape because they lack a cell wall.

Review Video: Difference Between Plant and Animal Cells
Visit mometrix.com/academy and enter code: 115568

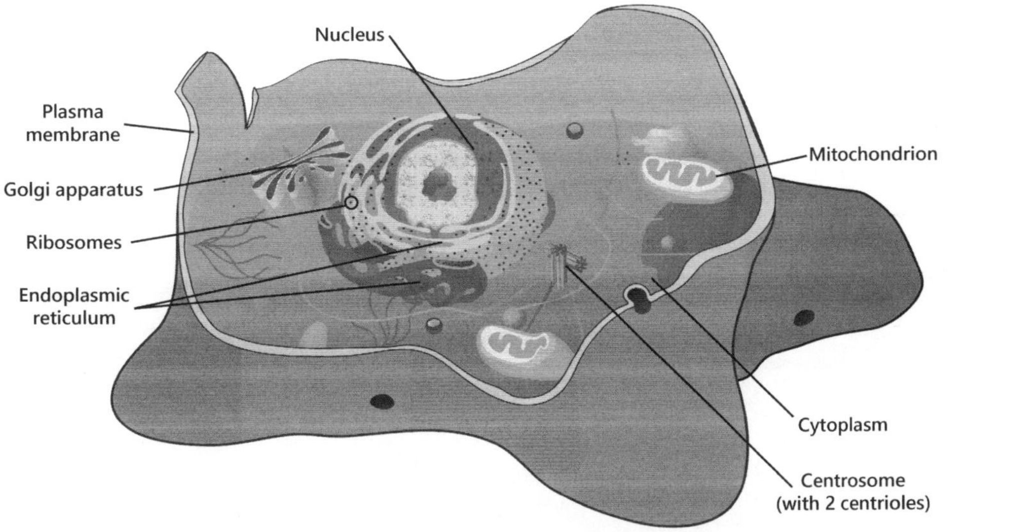

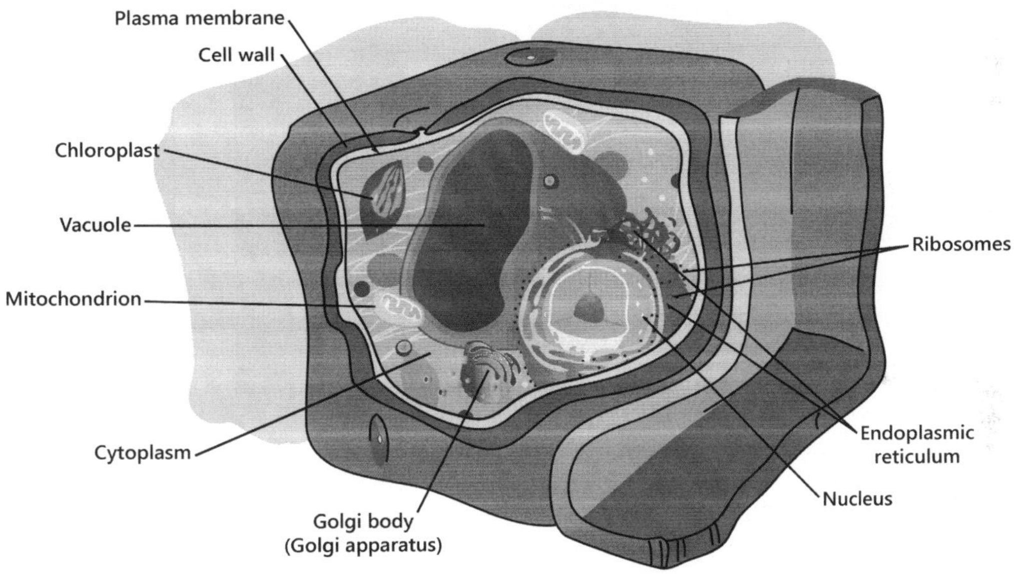

CELL MEMBRANES

The **cell membrane**, also referred to as the plasma membrane, is a thin semipermeable membrane of lipids and proteins. The cell membrane isolates the cell from its external environment while still enabling the cell to communicate with that outside environment. It consists of a phospholipid bilayer, or double layer, with the hydrophilic ("water-loving") ends of the outer layer facing the external environment, the inner layer facing the inside of the cell, and the hydrophobic ("water-fearing") ends facing each other. Cholesterol in the cell membrane adds stiffness and flexibility. Glycolipids help the cell to recognize other cells of the organisms. The proteins in the cell membrane help give the cells shape. Special proteins help the cell communicate with its external environment, while other proteins transport molecules across the cell membrane.

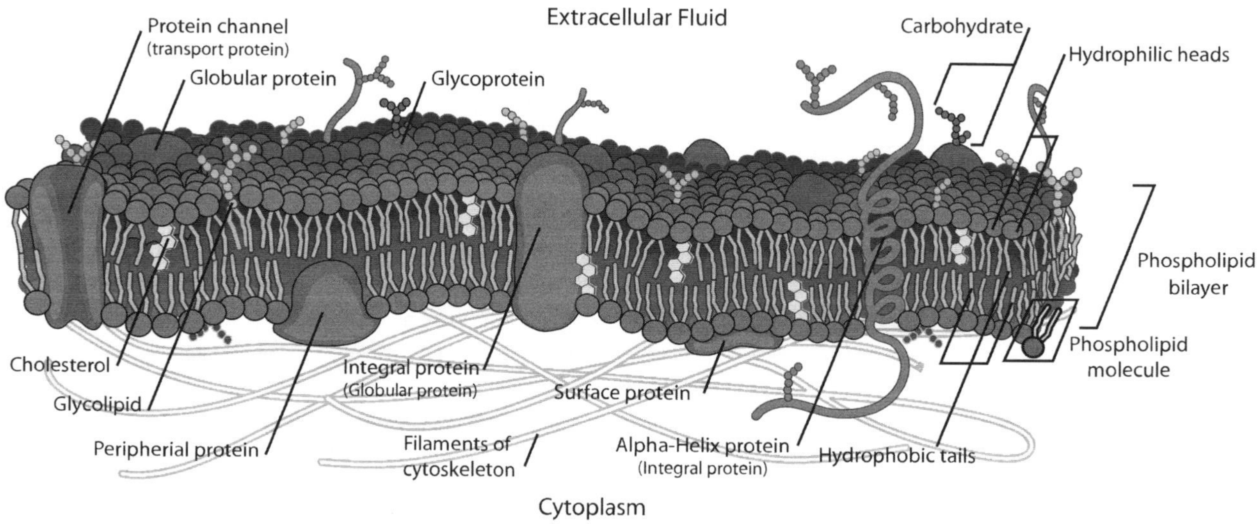

Review Video: Function of the Plasma Membrane
Visit mometrix.com/academy and enter code: 943095

NUCLEUS

Typically, a eukaryote has a single nucleus that takes up approximately 10% of the volume of the cell. Components of the nucleus include the nuclear envelope, nucleoplasm, chromatin, and nucleolus. The **nuclear envelope** is a double-layered membrane with the outer layer connected to the endoplasmic reticulum. The nucleus can communicate with the rest of the cell through several nuclear pores. The chromatin consists of deoxyribonucleic acid (DNA) and histones that are packaged into chromosomes during mitosis. The **nucleolus**, which is the dense central portion of the nucleus, produced and assembles ribosomes with the help of ribosomal RNA and proteins.

Functions of the nucleus include the storage of genetic material, production of ribosomes, and transcription of ribonucleic acid (RNA).

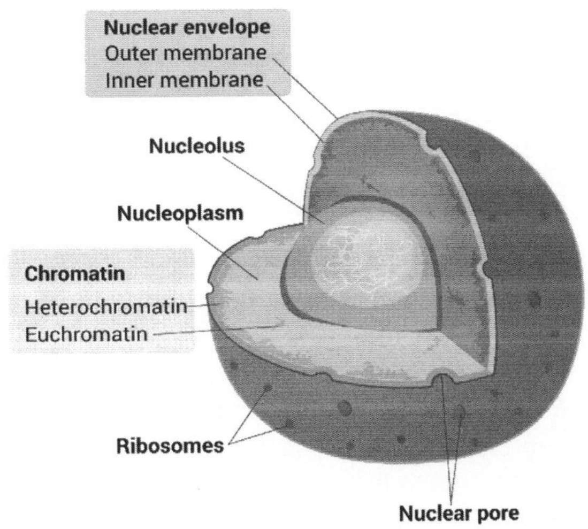

Review Video: Nucleic Acids
Visit mometrix.com/academy and enter code: 503931

Chloroplasts

Chloroplasts are large organelles that are enclosed in a double membrane. Just as cells contain a fluid called cytoplasm, chloroplasts contain a fluid called the **stroma**. Within the stroma, there are discs called **thylakoids**, which are arranged in stacks called **grana** (singular: granum). The thylakoids have chlorophyll molecules on their surfaces. **Stromal lamellae** separate the thylakoid stacks. Chloroplasts perform photosynthesis and make food (in the form of sugars) for the plant. The light reaction stage of photosynthesis occurs in the grana, and the dark reaction stage of photosynthesis occurs in the stroma. Sugars are formed in the stroma. Chloroplasts have their own DNA and can reproduce by fission independently.

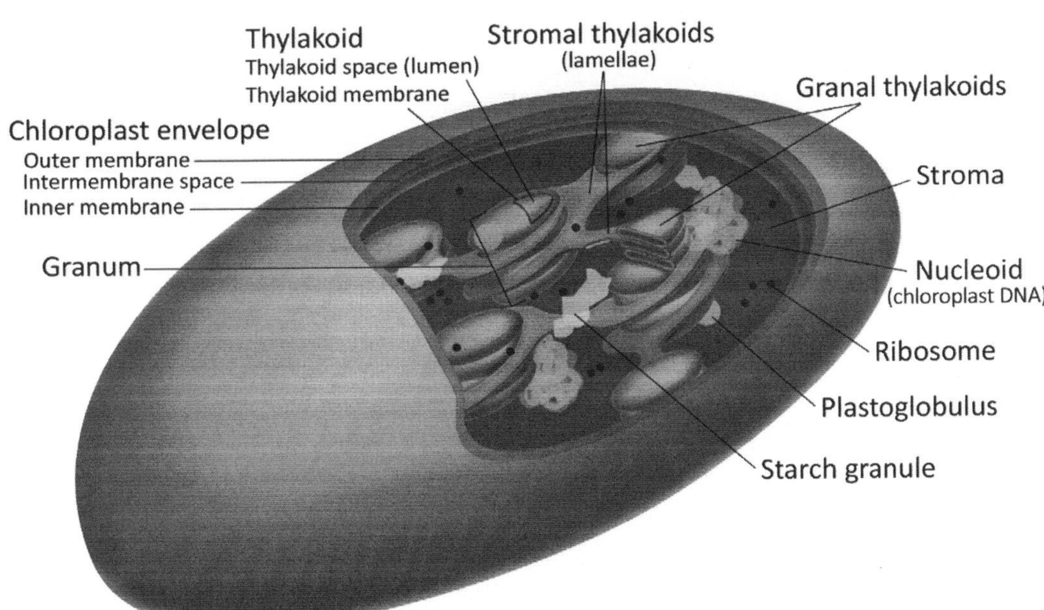

PLASTIDS

Plastids are major organelles found in plants and algae that are used to synthesize and store food. Because plastids can differentiate, there are many forms of plastids. Specialized plastids can store pigments, starches, fats, or proteins. Two examples of plastids are amyloplasts and chloroplasts. **Amyloplasts** are the plastids that store the starch formed from long chains of glucose produced during photosynthesis. Amyloplasts synthesize and store the starch granules through the polymerization of glucose. When needed, amyloplasts also convert these starch granules back into sugar. Fruits and potato tubers have large numbers of amyloplasts. **Chloroplasts** can synthesize and store starch. Interestingly, amyloplasts can redifferentiate and transform into chloroplasts.

MITOCHONDRIA

Mitochondria break down sugar molecules and produce energy in the form of molecules of adenosine triphosphate (ATP). Both plant and animal cells contain mitochondria. Mitochondria are enclosed in a bilayer semi-membrane of phospholipids and proteins. The intermembrane space is the space between the two layers. The outer membrane has proteins called porins, which allow small molecules through. The inner membrane contains proteins that aid in the synthesis of ATP. The matrix consists of enzymes that help synthesize ATP. Mitochondria have their own DNA and can reproduce by fission independently. Mitochondria also help to maintain calcium concentrations, form blood components and hormones, and are involved in activating cell death pathways.

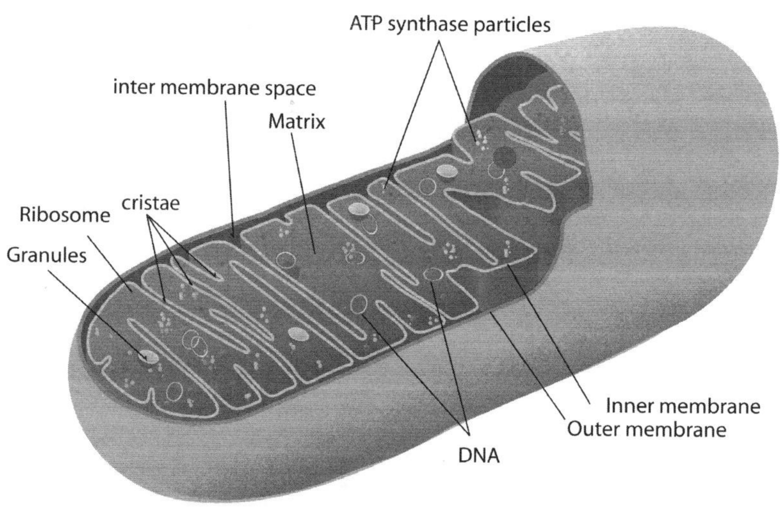

Review Video: Mitochondria
Visit mometrix.com/academy and enter code: 444287

RIBOSOMES

A **ribosome** consists of RNA and proteins. The RNA component of the ribosome is known as ribosomal RNA (rRNA). Ribosomes consist of two subunits, a large subunit and a small subunit. Few ribosomes are free in the cell. Most of the ribosomes in the cell are embedded in the rough endoplasmic reticulum located near the nucleus. Ribosomes are protein factories and translate the code of DNA into proteins by assembling long chains of amino acids. **Messenger RNA** (mRNA) is used by the ribosome to generate a specific protein sequence, while **transfer RNA** (tRNA) collects the needed amino acids and delivers them to the ribosome.

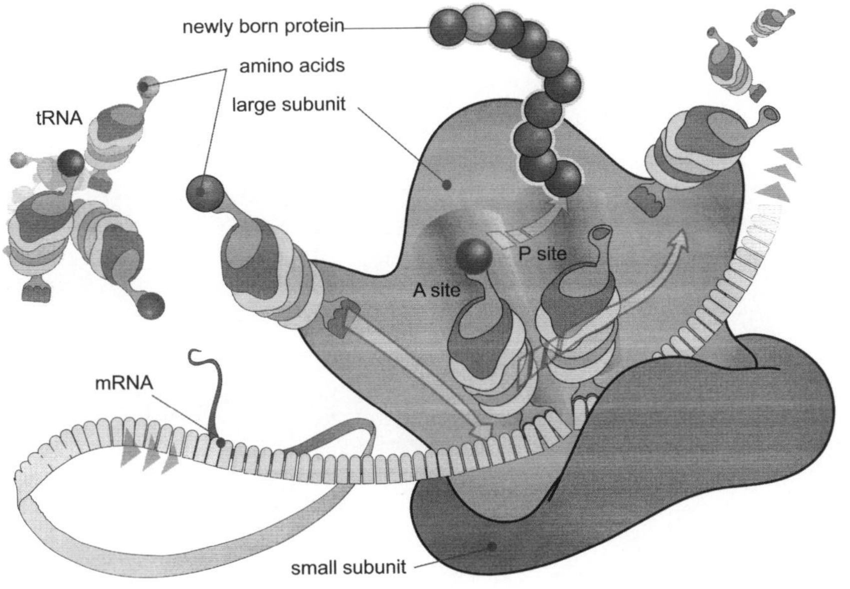

Golgi Apparatus

The **Golgi apparatus**, also called the Golgi body or Golgi complex, is a stack of flattened membranes called **cisternae** that package, ship, and distribute macromolecules such as carbohydrates, proteins, and lipids in shipping containers called **vesicles**. It also helps modify proteins and lipids before they are shipped. Most Golgi apparatuses have six to eight cisternae. Each Golgi apparatus has four regions: the cis region, the endo region, the medial region, and the trans region. Transfer vesicles from the rough endoplasmic reticulum (ER) enter at the cis region, and secretory vesicles leave the Golgi apparatus from the trans region.

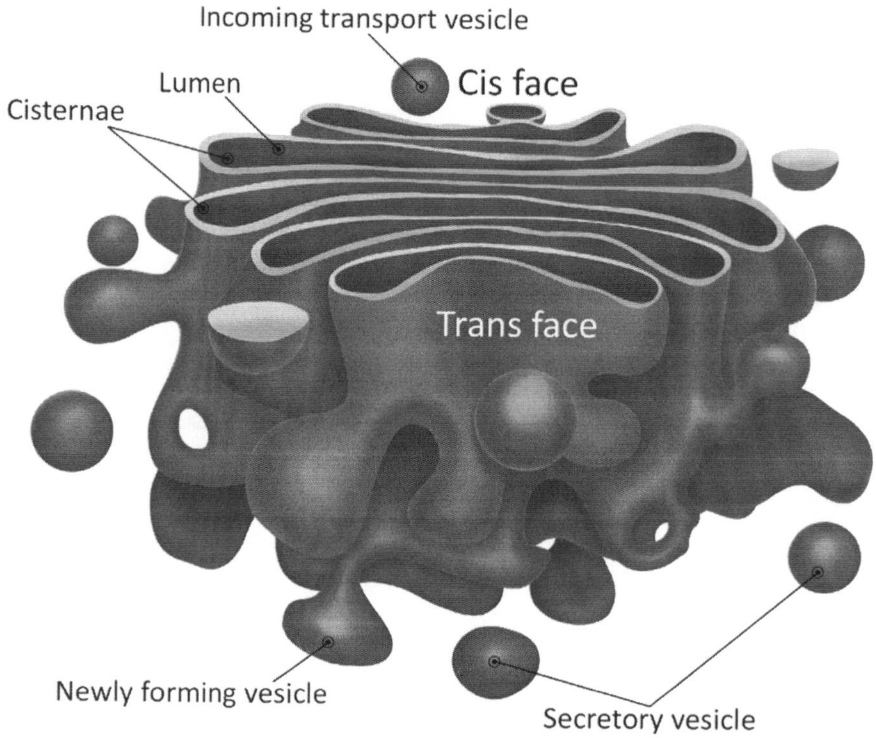

CYTOSKELETON

The **cytoskeleton** is a scaffolding system located in the cytoplasm. The cytoskeleton consists of elongated organelles made of proteins called microtubules, microfilaments, and intermediate filaments. These organelles provide shape, support, and the ability to move. These structures also assist in moving the chromosomes during mitosis. Microtubules and microfilaments help transport materials throughout the cell and are the major components in cilia and flagella.

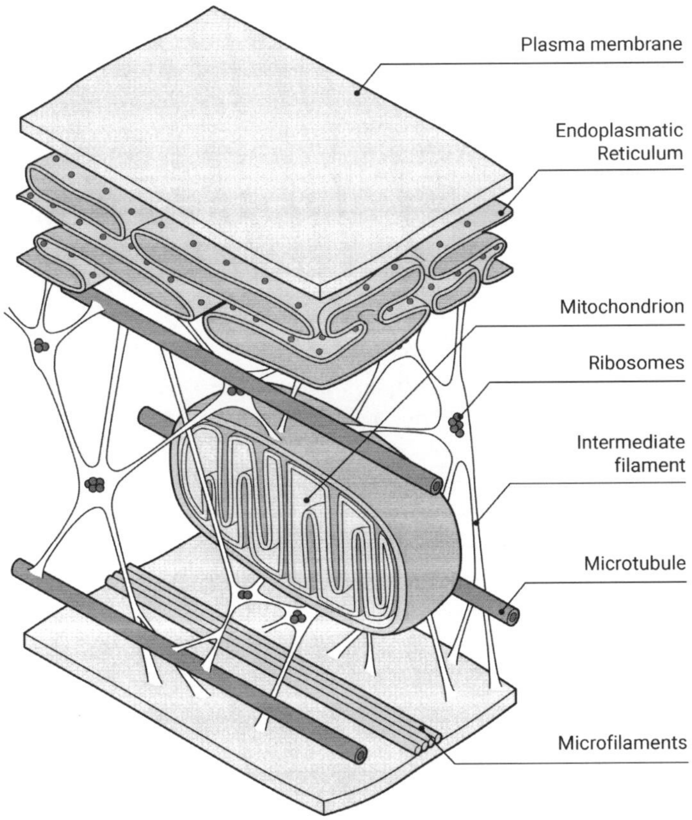

Chapter Quiz

Ready to see how well you retained what you just read? Scan the QR code to go directly to the chapter quiz interface for this study guide. If you're using a computer, simply visit the online resources page at **mometrix.com/resources719/ssreglivingenv** and click the Chapter Quizzes link.

Organismal Biology

Cell Cycle and Cellular Division

Cell Cycle Stages

The cell cycle consists of three stages: interphase, mitosis, and cytokinesis. **Interphase** is the longest stage of the cell cycle and involves the cell growing and making a copy of its DNA. Cells typically spend more than 90% of the cell cycle in interphase. Interphase includes two growth phases called G_1 and G_2. The order of interphase is the first growth cycle, **GAP 1** (G_1 phase), followed by the **synthesis phase** (S), and ending with the second growth phase, **GAP 2** (G_2 phase). During the G_1 phase of interphase, the cell increases the number of organelles by forming diploid cells. During the S phase of interphase, the DNA is replicated, and the chromosomes are doubled. During the G_2 phase of interphase, the cell synthesizes needed proteins and organelles, continues to increase in size, and prepares for mitosis. Once the G_2 phase ends, mitosis can begin.

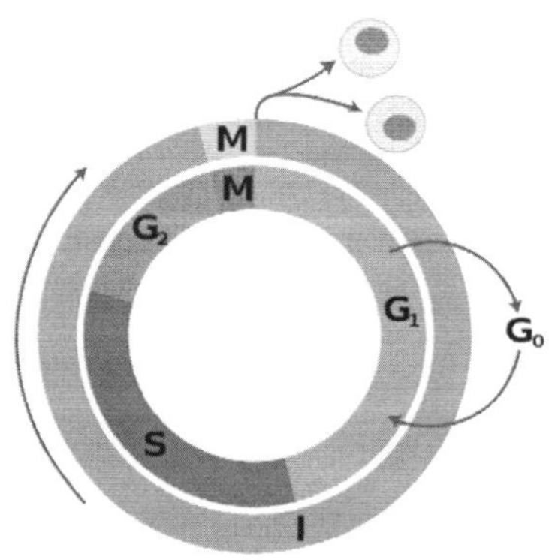

Mitosis

Mitosis is the asexual process of cell division. During mitosis, one parent cell divides into two identical daughter cells. Mitosis is used for growth, repair, and replacement of cells. Some unicellular organisms reproduce asexually by mitosis. Some multicellular organisms can reproduce by fragmentation or budding, which involves mitosis. Mitosis consists of four phases: prophase, metaphase, anaphase, and telophase. During **prophase**, the spindle fibers appear and the DNA is condensed and packaged as chromosomes that become visible. The nuclear membrane also breaks down, and the nucleolus disappears. During **metaphase**, the spindle apparatus is formed and the centromeres of the chromosomes line up on the equatorial plane. During **anaphase**, the centromeres divide and the two chromatids separate and are pulled toward the opposite poles of the cell. During **telophase**, the spindle fibers disappear, the nuclear membrane reforms, and the DNA in the chromatids is decondensed.

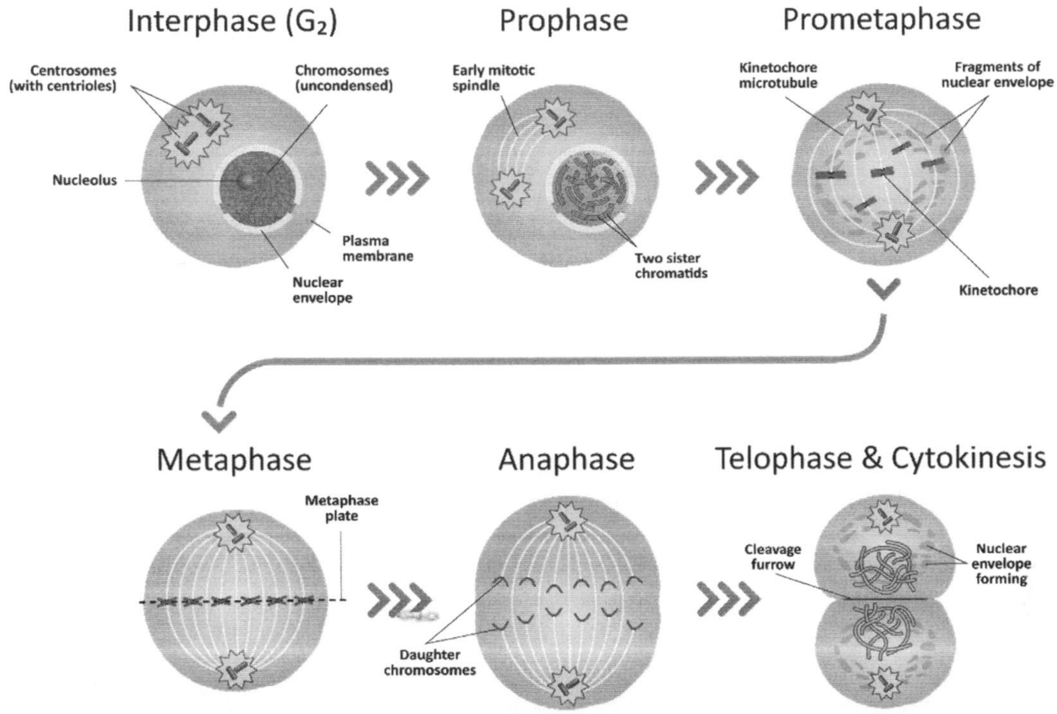

Review Video: Mitosis
Visit mometrix.com/academy and enter code: 849894

Cytokinesis

Cytokinesis is the dividing of the cytoplasm and cell membrane by the pinching of a cell into two new daughter cells at the end of mitosis. This occurs at the end of telophase when the actin filaments in the cytoskeleton form a contractile ring that narrows and divides the cell. In plant cells, a cell plate forms across the phragmoplast, which is the center of the spindle apparatus. In animal cells, as the contractile ring narrows, the cleavage furrow forms. Eventually, the contractile ring narrows down to the spindle apparatus joining the two cells and the cells eventually divide. Diagrams of the cleavage furrow of an animal cell and cell plate of a plant are shown below.

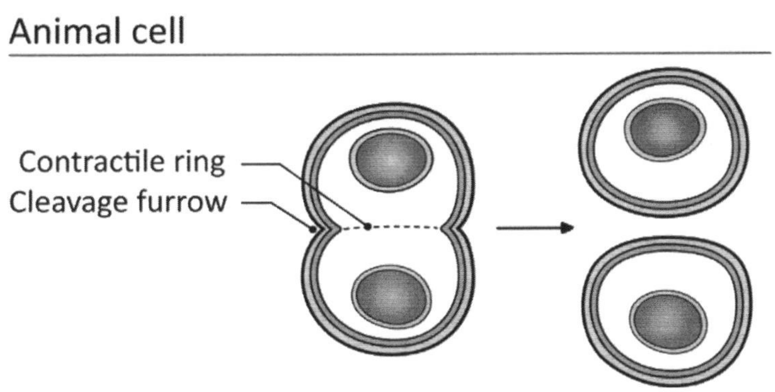

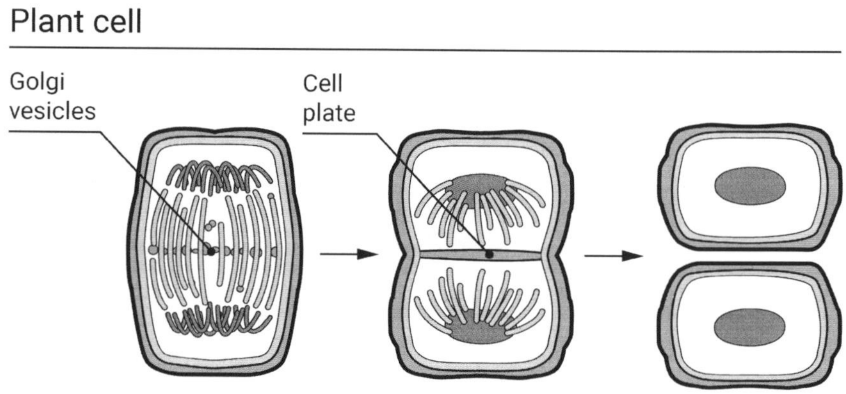

MEIOSIS

Meiosis is a type of cell division in which the number of chromosomes is reduced by half. Meiosis produces gametes, or egg and sperm cells. Meiosis occurs in two successive stages, which consist of a first mitotic division followed by a second mitotic division. During **meiosis I**, or the first meiotic division, the cell replicates its DNA in interphase and then continues through prophase I, metaphase I, anaphase I, and telophase I. At the end of meiosis I, there are two haploid daughter cells, each with half the number of chromosomes as the original diploid parent cell. Each chromosome consists of two sister chromatids, but these are considered a single chromosome. During **meiosis II**, the cell enters a brief interphase but does not replicate its DNA. Then, the cell continues through prophase II, metaphase II, anaphase II, and telophase II. During prophase II, the unduplicated chromosomes split. At the end of telophase II, there are four daughter cells that have half the number of chromosomes as the parent cell.

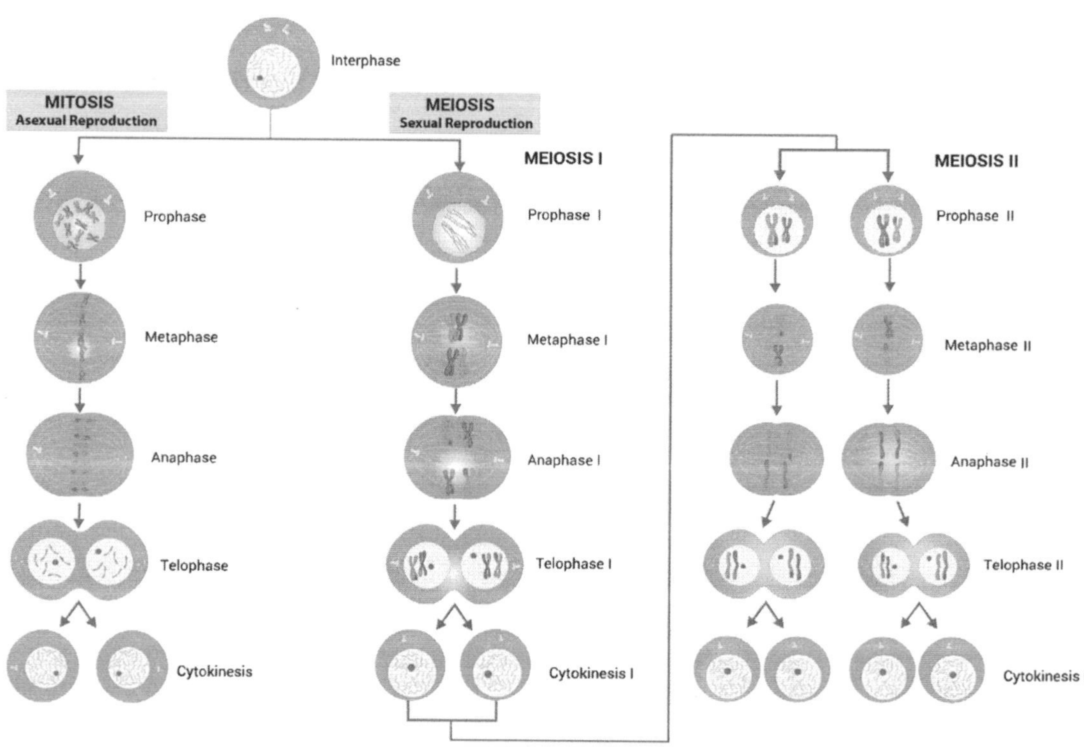

Cell Cycle Checkpoints

During the cell cycle, the cell goes through three checkpoints to ensure that the cell is dividing properly at each phase, that it is the appropriate time for division, and that the cell has not been damaged. The **first checkpoint** is at the end of the G_1 phase just before the cell undergoes the S phase, or synthesis. At this checkpoint, a cell may continue with cell division, delay the division, or rest. This **resting phase** is called G_0. In animal cells, the G_1 checkpoint is called **restriction.** Proteins called cyclin D and cyclin E, which are dependent on enzymes cyclin-dependent kinase 4 and cyclin-dependent kinase 2 (CDK4 and CDK2), respectively, largely control this first checkpoint. The **second checkpoint** is at the end of the G_2 phase just before the cell begins prophase during mitosis. The protein cyclin A, which is dependent on the enzyme CDK2, largely controls this checkpoint. During mitosis, the **third checkpoint** occurs at metaphase to check that the chromosomes are lined up along the equatorial plane. This checkpoint is largely controlled by cyclin B, which is dependent upon the enzyme CDK1.

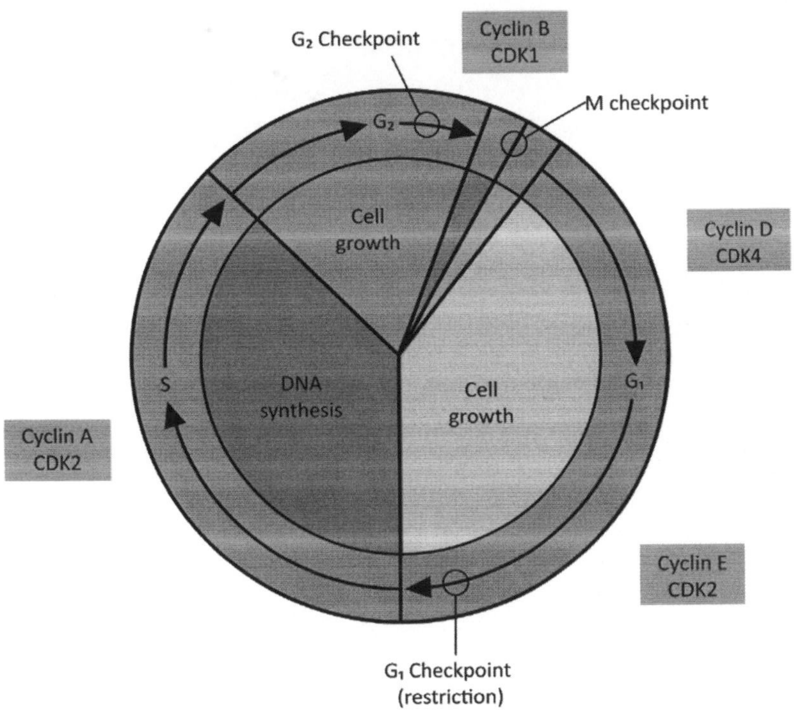

Mutations

Missense Mutations, Silent Mutations, and Nonsense Mutations

Mutations are changes in DNA sequences. **Point mutations** are changes in a single nucleotide in a DNA sequence. Three types of point mutations are missense, silent, and nonsense.

- **Missense mutations** result in a codon for a different amino acid. An example is mutating TGT (Cysteine codon) to TGG (Tryptophan codon).
- **Silent mutations** result in a codon for the same amino acid as the original sequence. An example is mutating TGT (Cysteine codon) to TGC (a different Cysteine codon).
- **Nonsense mutations** insert a premature stop codon, typically resulting in a non-functional protein. An example is mutating TGT (Cysteine codon) to TGA (STOP codon).

Review Video: Codons
Visit mometrix.com/academy and enter code: 978172

Frameshift Mutations and Inversion Mutations

Deletions and insertions can result in the addition of amino acids, the removal of amino acids, or cause a frameshift mutation. A **frameshift mutation** changes the reading frame of the mRNA (a new group of codons will be read), resulting in the formation of a new protein product. Mutations can also occur on the chromosomal level. For example, an **inversion** is when a piece of the chromosome inverts or flips its orientation.

Germline Mutations and Somatic Mutations

Mutations can occur in somatic (body) cells and germ cells (egg and sperm). **Somatic mutations** develop after conception and occur in an organism's body cells such as bone cells, liver cells, or brain cells. Somatic mutations cannot be passed on from parent to offspring. The mutation is limited to the specific descendent of the cell in which the mutation occurred. The mutation is not in the other body cells unless they are descendants of the originally mutated cell. Somatic mutations may cause cancer or diseases. Some somatic mutations are silent. **Germline mutations** are present at conception and occur in an organism's germ cells, which are only egg and sperms cells. Germline mutations may be passed on from parent to offspring. Germline mutations will be present in every cell of an offspring that inherits a germline mutation. Germline mutations may cause diseases. Some germline mutations are silent.

Mutagens

Mutagens are physical and chemical agents that cause changes or errors in DNA replication. Mutagens are external factors to an organism. Examples include ionizing radiation such as ultraviolet radiation, x-rays, and gamma radiation. Viruses and microorganisms that integrate their DNA into host chromosomes are also mutagens. Mutagens include environmental poisons such as asbestos, coal tars, tobacco, and benzene. Alcohol and diets high in fat have been shown to be mutagenic. Not all mutations are caused by mutagens. **Spontaneous mutations** can occur in DNA due to molecular decay.

Historical and Current Biological Classifications of Organisms

Historical and Current Kingdom Systems

In 1735 Carolus Linnaeus devised a two-kingdom classification system. He placed all living things into either the *Animalia* kingdom or the *Plantae* kingdom. Fungi and algae were classified as plants. Also, Linnaeus developed the binomial nomenclature system that is still used today. In 1866, Ernst Haeckel introduced a three-kingdom classification system, adding the *Protista* kingdom to Linnaeus's animal and plant kingdoms. Bacteria were classified as protists and cyanobacteria were still classified as plants. In 1938, Herbert Copeland introduced a four-kingdom classification system in which bacteria and cyanobacteria were moved to the *Monera* kingdom. In 1969, Robert Whittaker introduced a five-kingdom system that moved fungi from the plant kingdom to the *Fungi* kingdom. Some algae were still classified as plants. In 1977, Carl Woese introduced a six-kingdom system in which in the *Monera* kingdom was replaced with the *Eubacteria* kingdom and the *Archaebacteria* kingdom.

How animals are classified

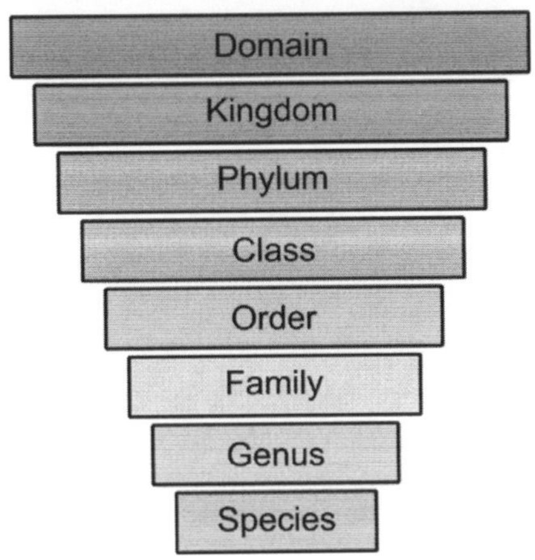

Domain Classification System

In 1990, Carl Woese introduced his domain classification system. **Domains** are broader groupings above the kingdom level. This system consists of three domains—*Archaea*, *Bacteria*, and *Eukarya*. All eukaryotes such as plants, animals, fungi, and protists are classified in the *Eukarya* domain. The *Bacteria* and *Archaea* domains consist of prokaryotes. Organisms previously classified in the *Monera* kingdom are now classified into either the *Bacteria* or *Archaea* domain based on their ribosomal RNA structure. Members of the *Archaea* domain often live in extremely harsh environments.

Review Video: Biological Classification Systems
Visit mometrix.com/academy and enter code: 736052

Viruses, Bacteria, Protists, Fungi, Plants, and Animals

Viruses

Viruses are nonliving, infectious particles that act as parasites in living organisms. Viruses are acellular, which means that they lack cell structure. Viruses cannot reproduce outside of living cells. The structure of a virus is a nucleic acid genome, which may be either DNA or RNA, surrounded by a protective protein coat or **capsid**. In some viruses, the capsid may be surrounded by a lipid membrane or envelope. Viruses can contain up to 500 genes and have various shapes. They usually are too small to be seen without the aid of an electron microscope. Viruses can infect plants, animals, fungi, protists, and bacteria. Viruses can attack only specific types of cells that have specific receptors on their surfaces. Viruses do not divide or reproduce like living cells. Instead, they use the host cell they infect by "reprogramming" it, using the nucleic acid genome, to make more copies of the virus. The host cell usually bursts to release these copies.

Review Video: Viruses and Antiviral Drugs
Visit mometrix.com/academy and enter code: 984455

Bacteria

Bacteria are small, prokaryotic, single-celled organisms. Bacteria have a circular loop of DNA (plasmid) that is not contained within a nuclear membrane. Bacterial ribosomes are not bound to the endoplasmic reticulum, as in eukaryotes. A cell wall containing peptidoglycan surrounds the bacterial plasma membrane. Some bacteria such as pathogens are further encased in a gel-like, sticky layer called the **capsule**, which enhances their ability to cause disease. Bacteria can be autotrophs or heterotrophs. Some bacterial heterotrophs are saprophytes that function as decomposers in ecosystems. Many types of bacteria share commensal or mutualistic relationships with other organisms. Most bacteria reproduce asexually by binary fission. Two identical daughter cells are produced from one parent cell. Some bacteria can transfer genetic material to other bacteria through a process called conjugation, while some bacteria can incorporate DNA from the environment in a process called transformation.

Protists

Protists are small, eukaryotic, single-celled organisms. Although protists are small, they are much larger than prokaryotic bacteria. Protists have three general forms, which include plantlike protists, animal-like protists, and fungus-like protists. **Plantlike protists** are algae that contain chlorophyll and perform photosynthesis. Animal-like protists are **protozoa** with no cell walls that typically lack chlorophyll and are grouped by their method of locomotion, which may use flagella, cilia, or a different structure. **Fungus-like protists**, which do not have chitin in their cell walls, are generally grouped as either slime molds or water molds. Protists may be autotrophic or heterotrophic. Autotrophic protists include many species of algae, while heterotrophic protists include parasitic, commensal, and mutualistic protozoa. Slime molds are heterotrophic fungus-like protists, which consume microorganisms. Some protists reproduce sexually, but most reproduce asexually by binary fission. Some reproduce asexually by spores while others reproduce by alternation of generations and require two hosts in their life cycle.

Fungi

Fungi are nonmotile organisms with eukaryotic cells and contain chitin in their cell walls. Most fungi are multicellular, but a few including yeast are unicellular. Fungi have multicellular filaments called **hyphae** that are grouped together into the mycelium. Fungi do not perform photosynthesis and are considered heterotrophs. Fungi can be parasitic, mutualistic or free living. Free-living fungi include mushrooms and toadstools. Parasitic fungi include fungi responsible for ringworm and athlete's foot. Mycorrhizae are mutualistic fungi that live in or near plant roots increasing the roots' surface area of absorption. Almost all fungi reproduce asexually by spores, but most fungi also have a sexual phase in the production of spores. Some fungi reproduce by budding or fragmentation.

> **Review Video: Feeding Among Heterotrophs**
> Visit mometrix.com/academy and enter code: 836017

Plants

Plants are multicellular organisms with eukaryotic cells containing cellulose in their cell walls. Plant cells have chlorophyll and perform photosynthesis. Plants can be vascular or nonvascular. **Vascular plants** have true leaves, stems, and roots that contain xylem and phloem. **Nonvascular plants** lack true leaves, stems and roots and do not have any true vascular tissue but instead rely on diffusion and osmosis to transport most of materials or resources needed to survive. Almost all plants are autotrophic, relying on photosynthesis for food. A small number do not have chlorophyll and are parasitic, but these are extremely rare. Plants can reproduce sexually or asexually. Many plants reproduce by seeds produced in the fruits of the plants, while some plants reproduce by seeds on cones. One type of plant, ferns, reproduce by a different system that utilizes spores. Some plants can even reproduce asexually by vegetative reproduction.

> **Review Video: Kingdom Plantae**
> Visit mometrix.com/academy and enter code: 710084

Structure, Organization, Modes of Nutrition, and Reproduction of Animals

Animals are multicellular organism with eukaryotic cells that do not have cell walls surrounding their plasma membranes. Animals have several possible structural body forms. Animals can be relatively simple in structure such as sponges, which do not have a nervous system. Other animals are more complex with cells organized into tissues, and tissues organized into organs, and organs even further organized into systems. Invertebrates such as arthropods, nematodes, and annelids have complex body systems. Vertebrates including fish, amphibians, reptiles, birds, and mammals are the most complex with detailed systems such as those with gills, air sacs, or lungs designed to exchange respiratory gases. All animals are heterotrophs and obtain their nutrition by consuming autotrophs or other heterotrophs. Most animals are motile, but some animals move their environment to bring food to them. All animals reproduce sexually at some point in their life cycle. Typically, this involves the union of a sperm and egg to produce a zygote.

Characteristics of the Major Animal Phyla

Characteristics of the Major Animal Phyla

Body Planes

Animals can exhibit bilateral symmetry, radial symmetry, or asymmetry. With **bilateral symmetry**, the organism can be cut in half along only one plane to produce two identical halves. Most animals, including all vertebrates such as mammals, birds, reptiles, amphibians, and fish, exhibit bilateral symmetry. Many invertebrates including arthropods and crustaceans also exhibit bilateral symmetry. With **radial symmetry**, the organism can be cut in half along several planes to produce two identical halves. Starfish, sea urchins, and jellyfish exhibit radial symmetry. With **asymmetry**, the organism exhibits no symmetry. Very few organisms in the animal phyla exhibit asymmetry, but a few species of sponges are asymmetrical.

Body Cavities

Animals can be grouped based on their types of body cavities. A **coelom** is a fluid-filled body cavity between the alimentary canal and the body wall. The three body plans based on the formation of the coelom are coelomates, pseudocoelomates, and acoelomates. **Coelomates** have a true coelom located within the mesoderm. Most animals including arthropods, mollusks, annelids, echinoderms, and chordates are coelomates. **Pseudocoelomates** have a body cavity called a pseudocoelom. **Pseudocoeloms** are not considered true coeloms. Pseudocoeloms are located between mesoderm and endoderm instead of actually in the mesoderm as in a true coelom. Pseudocoelomates include roundworms and rotifers. **Acoelomates** do not have body cavities. Simple or primitive animals such as sponges, jellyfish, sea anemones, hydras, flatworms, and ribbon worms are acoelomates.

Modes of Reproduction

Animals can reproduce sexually or asexually. Most animals reproduce sexually. In **sexual reproduction**, males and females have different reproductive organs that produce **gametes**. Males have testes that produce sperm, and females have ovaries that produce eggs. During fertilization, a sperm cell unites with an egg cell, forming a **zygote**. Fertilization can occur internally such as in most mammals and birds or externally such as aquatic animals such as fish and frogs. The zygote undergoes cell division, which develops into an embryo and eventually develops into an adult organism. Some embryos develop in eggs such as in fish, amphibians, reptiles, and birds. Some mammals are **oviparous** meaning that they lay eggs, but most are **viviparous** meaning they have a uterus in which the embryo develops. One particular type of mammal called **marsupials** give birth to an immature fetus that finishes development in a pouch. However, there are some animals reproduce **asexually**. For example, hydras reproduce by budding, and starfish and planarians can reproduce by fragmentation and regeneration. Some fish, frogs, and insects can even reproduce by parthenogenesis, which is a type of self-reproduction without fertilization.

Modes of Temperature Regulation

Animals can be classified as either homeotherms or poikilotherms. **Homeotherms**, also called warm-blooded animals or **endotherms**, maintain a constant body temperature regardless of the temperature of the environment. Homeotherms such as mammals and birds have a high metabolic rate because a lot of energy is needed to maintain the constant temperature. **Poikilotherms**, also called cold-blooded animals or **ectotherms**, do not maintain a constant body temperature. Their body temperature fluctuates with the temperature of the environment. Poikilotherms such as arthropods, fish, amphibians, and reptiles have metabolic rates that fluctuate with their body temperature.

Hierarchy of Multicellular Organisms

Organizational Hierarchy within Multicellular Organisms

Cells are the smallest living units of organisms. Tissues are groups of cells that work together to perform a specific function. Organs are groups of tissues that work together to perform a specific function. Organ systems are groups of organs that work together to perform a specific function. An organism is an individual that contains several body systems.

Cells

Cells are the basic structural units of all living things. Cells are composed of various molecules including proteins, carbohydrates, lipids, and nucleic acids. All animal cells are eukaryotic and have a nucleus, cytoplasm, and a cell membrane. Organelles include mitochondria, ribosomes, endoplasmic reticulum, Golgi apparatuses, and vacuoles. Specialized cells are numerous, including but not limited to, muscle cells, nerve cells, epithelial cells, bone cells, blood cells, and cartilage cells. Cells can be grouped together in tissues to perform specific functions.

TISSUES

Tissues are groups of cells that work together to perform a specific function. Tissues can be grouped into four broad categories: muscle tissue, connective tissue, nerve tissue, and epithelial tissue. Muscle tissue is involved in body movement. **Muscle tissues** can be composed of skeletal muscle cells, cardiac muscle cells, or smooth muscle cells. Skeletal muscles include the muscles commonly called biceps, triceps, hamstrings, and quadriceps. Cardiac muscle tissue is found only in the heart. Smooth muscle tissue provides tension in the blood vessels, controls pupil dilation, and aids in peristalsis. **Connective tissues** include bone tissue, cartilage, tendons, ligaments, fat, blood, and lymph. **Nerve tissue** is located in the brain, spinal cord, and nerves. **Epithelial tissue** makes up the layers of the skin and various membranes. Tissues are grouped together as organs to perform specific functions.

ORGANS AND ORGAN SYSTEMS

Organs are groups of tissues that work together to perform specific functions. **Organ systems** are groups of organs that work together to perform specific functions. Complex animals have several organs that are grouped together in multiple systems. In mammals, there are 11 major organ systems: integumentary system, respiratory system, cardiovascular system, endocrine system, nervous system, immune system, digestive system, excretory system, muscular system, skeletal system, and reproductive system.

Human Anatomy and Physiology

BODY SYSTEMS

Functions of the human body can be divided into the following body systems.

- **Cardiovascular**: Pumps blood throughout the body via the heart and blood vessels
- **Respiratory**: Regulates gas exchange (oxygen intake and carbon dioxide expulsion)
- **Digestive**: Transforms food into energy and eliminates solid waste
- **Urinary**: Removes waste and toxins from the blood and expels them from the body through urine
- **Endocrine**: Releases hormones into the bloodstream to control metabolism, growth, and reproduction
- **Immune and Lymphatic Systems**: Defends against all foreign substances
- **Integumentary**: Skin prevents moisture loss, regulates temperature, protects from sunburn, and senses pain, pressure, touch, hot and cold
- **Musculoskeletal**: Skeletal muscles move the body, smooth muscles control the physical functioning of internal organs, and cardiac muscle pumps blood. The skeleton supports and shapes, protects internal organs, stores minerals, and produces blood cells
- **Nervous**: Controls movement, memory, and senses and communicates with the outside world
- **Reproductive**: Allows continuation of the human species through reproduction and childbearing and differentiates the sexes

Note that different models may have overlapping approaches to the body systems. For instance, the excretory system is not listed above, but the functions of the excretory systems overlap and are covered by the urinary and digestive systems.

The Three Primary Body Planes

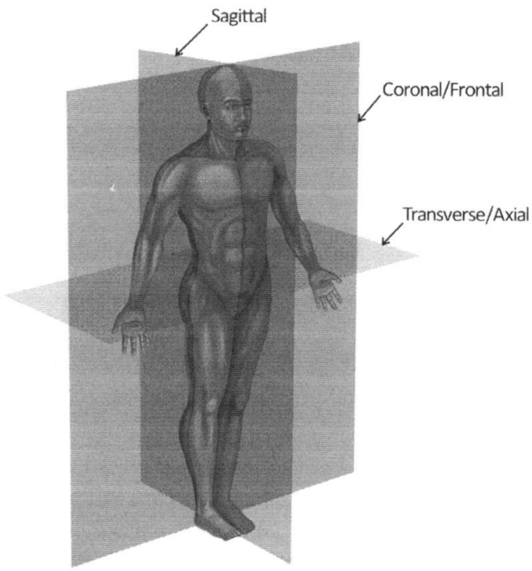

- The **transverse (or horizontal) plane** divides the patient's body into imaginary upper (*superior*) and lower (*inferior or caudal*) halves.
- The **sagittal plane** divides the body, or any body part, vertically into right and left sections. The sagittal plane runs parallel to the midline of the body.
- The **coronal (or frontal) plane** divides the body, or any body structure, vertically into front and back (*anterior* and *posterior*) sections. The coronal plane runs vertically through the body at right angles to the midline.

Terms of Direction

- **Medial** means *nearer to the midline* of the body. In anatomical position, the little finger is medial to the thumb.
- **Lateral** is the opposite of medial. It refers to structures *further away from the body's midline*, at the sides. In anatomical position, the thumb is lateral to the little finger.
- **Proximal** refers to structures *closer to the center* of the body. The hip is proximal to the knee.
- **Distal** refers to structures *further away from the center* of the body. The knee is distal to the hip.
- **Anterior** refers to structures in *front.*
- **Posterior** refers to structures *behind.*
- **Cephalad** and **cephalic** are adverbs meaning towards the *head.* **Cranial** is the adjective, meaning of the *skull.*
- **Caudad** is an adverb meaning towards the *tail* or posterior. **Caudal** is the adjective, meaning of the *hindquarters.*
- **Superior** means *above*, or closer to the head.
- **Inferior** means *below*, or closer to the feet.

Cardiovascular System

The main functions of the **cardiovascular system** are gas exchange, the delivery of nutrients and hormones, and waste removal. The cardiovascular system consists primarily of the heart, blood, and blood vessels. The **heart** is a pump that pushes blood through the arteries. **Arteries** are blood vessels that carry blood away from the heart, and **veins** are blood vessels that carry blood back to the heart. The exchange of materials between blood and cells occur in the **capillaries**, which are the smallest of the blood vessels.

Review Video: Functions of the Circulatory System
Visit mometrix.com/academy and enter code: 376581

Review Video: Mnemonics for Heart Anatomy and Physiology
Visit mometrix.com/academy and enter code: 849489

Review Video: Electrical Conduction System of the Heart
Visit mometrix.com/academy and enter code: 624557

Review Video: How the Heart Functions
Visit mometrix.com/academy and enter code: 569724

Heart Chambers and Valves

There are four chambers of the heart that have valves separating them and regulating a one-way flow of blood between the chambers.

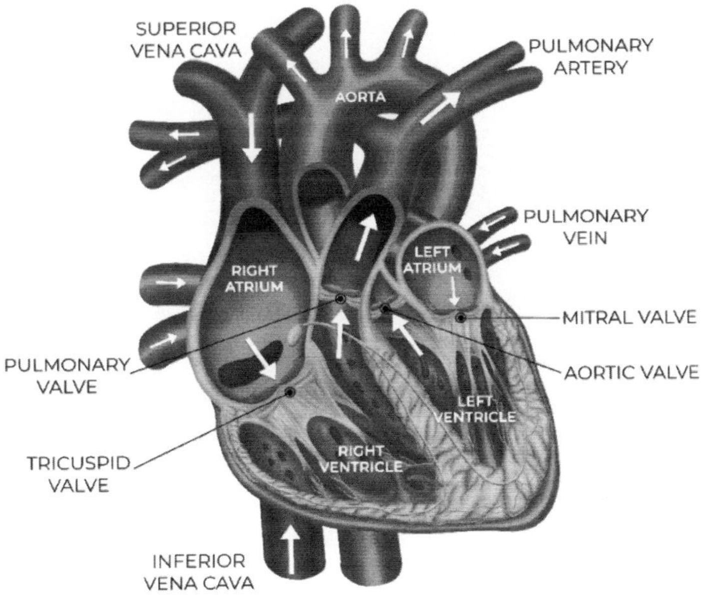

RESPIRATORY SYSTEM

The primary function of the **respiratory system** is to move air in and out of the body in order to facilitate the exchange of oxygen and carbon dioxide. The respiratory system consists of the nasal passages, pharynx, larynx, trachea, bronchial tubes, lungs, and diaphragm. **Bronchial tubes** branch into **bronchioles**, which end in clusters of alveoli. The **alveoli** are tiny sacs inside the lungs where gas exchange takes place. When the **diaphragm** contracts, the volume of the chest increases, which reduces the pressure in the **lungs**. Then, air is inhaled through the nose or mouth and passes through the pharynx, larynx, trachea, and bronchial tubes into the lungs. When the diaphragm relaxes, the volume in the chest cavity decreases, forcing the air out of the lungs. The respiratory system works jointly with the **cardiovascular system** by taking **oxygenated blood** (red blood cells) and distributing them through arteries and capillaries. **Deoxygenated blood** (carbon dioxide) is transported via the venous system back to the lungs to exhaled. The respiratory system also functions to enhance speech and smell.

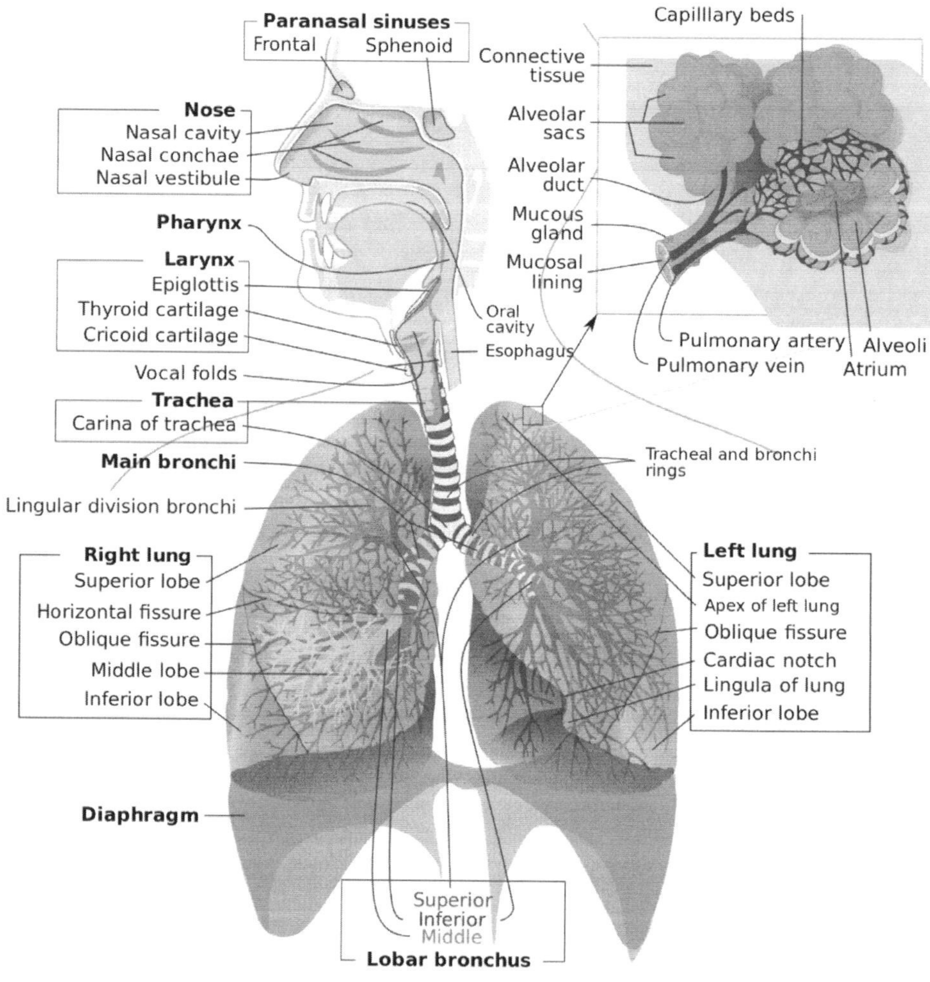

> **Review Video: Respiratory System**
> Visit mometrix.com/academy and enter code: 783075
>
> **Review Video: Pulmonary Circuit**
> Visit mometrix.com/academy and enter code: 955608

DIGESTIVE SYSTEM

The main function of the **digestive system** is to process the food that is consumed by an organism. This includes mechanical and chemical processing. Depending on the organism, **mechanical processes**, or the physical process of breaking food into smaller pieces, can happen in various ways. Mammals have teeth to chew their food, while many animals such as birds, earthworms, crocodilians, and crustaceans have a gizzard or gizzard-like organ that grinds their food. **Chemical digestion** includes breaking food into simpler nutrients that the body can use for specific processes. While chewing, saliva (which contains special enzymes) is secreted to begin the breakdown of starches. Many animals such as mammals, birds, reptiles, amphibians, and fish have a stomach that stores and absorbs food. Gastric juice containing enzymes and hydrochloric acid is mixed with the food. The intestine or intestines absorb nutrients and reabsorb water from the undigested material. Additionally, many animals have a liver, gallbladder, and pancreas, which aid in digestion of proteins and fats. Undigested wasted are eliminated from the body through an anus or cloaca.

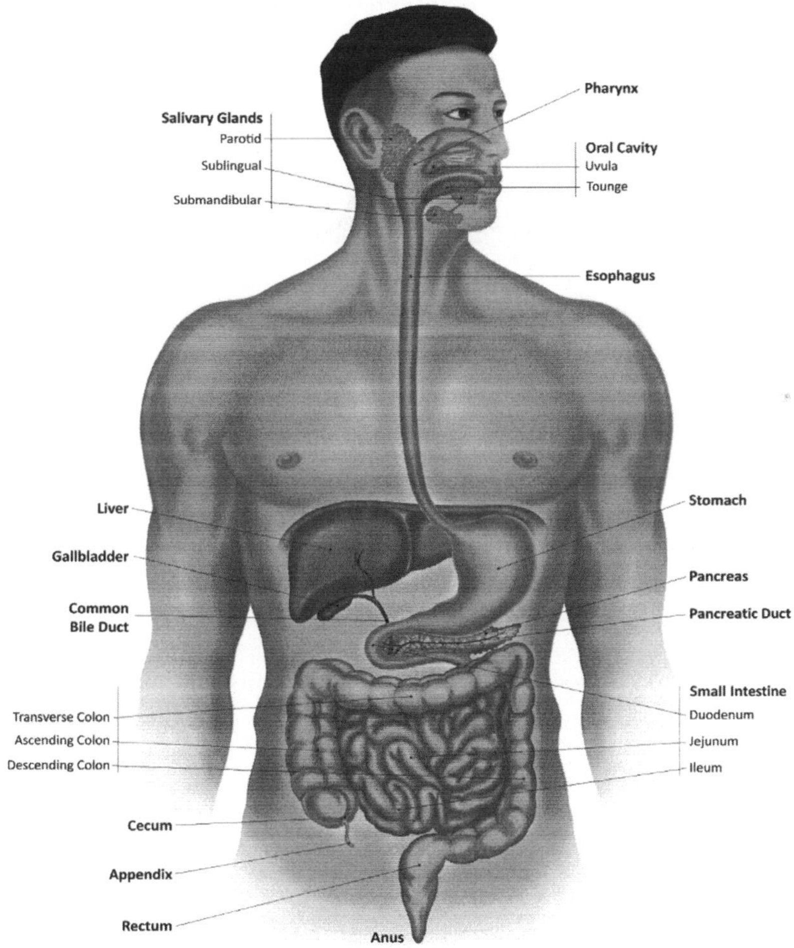

Review Video: Gastrointestinal System
Visit mometrix.com/academy and enter code: 378740

Urinary System

The **urinary system** consists of the bladder, kidneys, ureter, and urethra. Their main function is to eliminate waste products by expelling urine. This system also maintains homeostatic balance of water by excreting excess urine, maintaining electrolytes in the blood stream, and regulating blood Ph levels. This balance of water is crucial to body functioning as dehydration can lead to low blood pressure, which in turn can result in metabolic shock. **Metabolic shock** is characterized by low blood pressure that affects the kidneys, liver, and brain. **Dehydration** can also affect the muscular, system resulting in cramps from poor thermal regulation and altered fluid movement across tissue membranes.

Kidneys

The **kidneys** are involved in blood filtration, pH balance, and the reabsorption of nutrients to maintain proper blood volume and ion balance. The **nephron** is the working unit of the kidney. The parts of the nephron include the glomerulus, Bowman's capsule, and loop of Henle. Filtration takes place in the nephron's **glomerulus.** Water and dissolved materials such as glucose and amino acids pass on into the Bowman's capsule. Depending on concentration gradients, water and dissolved materials can pass back into the blood primarily through the proximal convoluted tubule. Reabsorption and water removal occurs in the **loop of Henle** and the conducting duct. Urine and other nitrogenous wastes pass from the kidneys to the bladders and are expelled.

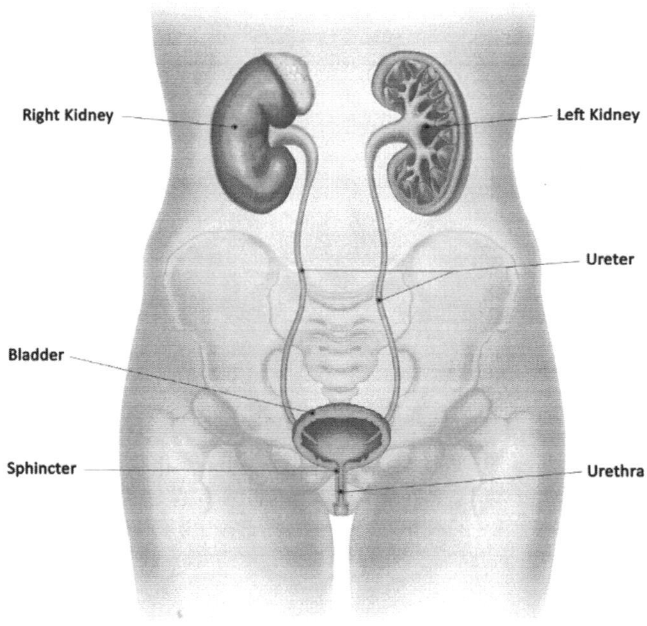

Review Video: Urinary System
Visit mometrix.com/academy and enter code: 601053

ENDOCRINE SYSTEM

The **endocrine system** consists of several ductless glands, which secrete hormones directly into the bloodstream. The **pituitary gland** controls the functions of the other glands in the system, regulates skeletal growth, and initiates the development of reproductive organs. The **pineal gland** regulates sleep cycles. The **thyroid gland** regulates metabolism and work with the **parathyroid glands** to help regulate the calcium level in the blood. The **adrenal glands** secrete the emergency hormone epinephrine, stimulate body repairs, and regulate sodium and potassium levels in the blood. The **islets of Langerhans**, located in the pancreas, secrete insulin and glucagon to regulate the level of blood sugar. In females, **ovaries** produce estrogen, which stimulates sexual development, and progesterone, which functions during pregnancy. In males, the **testes** secrete testosterone, which stimulates sexual development and sperm production.

Gland	Hormones	Disease
Adrenal Cortex	Aldosterone Cortisol Androgens	Addison's Disease Cushing's Disease
Adrenal Medulla	Epinephrine Norepinephrine	Anxiety Attacks Depression
Anterior Pituitary	Adrenocorticotropic hormone (ACTH) Follicle-stimulating hormone (FSH) Gonadotropic hormones Growth hormone (GH) Luteinizing hormone (LH) Prolactin Thyroid Stimulating Hormone (TSH)	Dwarfism Gigantism
Hypothalamus/ Posterior Pituitary	Inhibiting hormones (stop the release of other hormones) Antidiuretic hormone (ADH) Oxytocin Releasing hormones (trigger the release of other hormones)	Diabetes Insipidus
Kidneys	Calcitriol Erythropoietin	Hypertension
Ovaries	Estrogen Progesterone	Endometriosis Menometrorrhagia
Pancreas	Insulin Glucagon	Diabetes Mellitus
Parathyroid	Parathyroid hormone	Tetany Renal calculi
Pineal	Melatonin	Alzheimer's Disease
Testes	Testosterone	Gynecomastia Klinefelter Syndrome
Thymus	Thymic factor (TF) Thymosin Thymic humoral factor (THF) Thymopoietin	DiGeorge Syndrome

Gland	Hormones	Disease
Thyroid	Calcitonin Thyroxine (T4) Triiodothyronine (T3)	Cretinism Hypo/Hyperthyroidism Goiter Myxedema
Digestive tract	Gastrin Cholecystokinin Secretin Ghrelin Motilin	Gastritis Gastroesophageal reflux

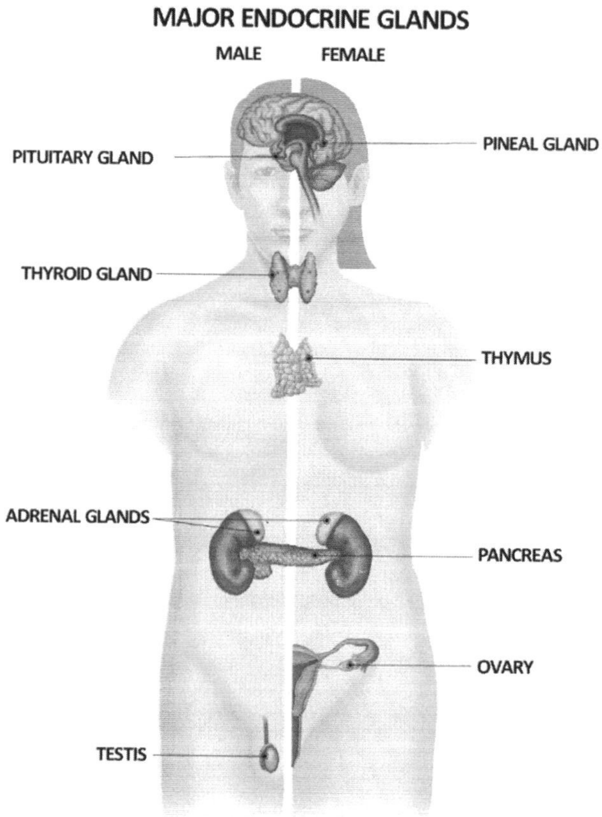

Review Video: Endocrine System
Visit mometrix.com/academy and enter code: 678939

Immune and Lymphatic Systems

Immune System

The **immune system** in animals defends the body against infection and disease. The immune system can be divided into two broad categories: innate immunity and adaptive immunity. **Innate immunity** includes the skin and mucous membranes, which provide a physical barrier to prevent pathogens from entering the body. Special chemicals including enzymes and proteins in mucus, tears, sweat, and stomach juices destroy pathogens. Numerous white blood cells such as neutrophils and macrophages protect the body from invading pathogens. **Adaptive immunity** involves the body responding to a specific antigen. Typically, B-lymphocytes or B cells produce antibodies against a specific antigen, and T-lymphocytes or T-cells take special roles as helpers, regulators, or killers. Some T-cells function as memory cells.

Review Video: Immune System
Visit mometrix.com/academy and enter code: 622899

Lymphatic System

The **lymphatic system** is connected to the cardiovascular system through a network of capillaries. The lymphatic system filters out organisms that cause disease, controls the production of disease-fighting antibodies, and produces white blood cells. The lymphatic system also prevents body tissues from swelling by draining fluids from them. Two of the most important areas in this system are the right lymphatic duct and the thoracic duct. The **right lymphatic duct** moves the immunity-bolstering lymph fluid through the top half of the body, while the **thoracic duct** moves lymph throughout the lower half. The spleen, thymus, and lymph nodes all generate and store the chemicals which form lymph and which are essential to protecting the body from disease.

The **lymphatic system** consists of the **thymus**, **lymph nodes**, **bone marrow**, and **spleen**. They primarily serve to distribute filtered fluids throughout the body and to remove excess fluid and debris. **White blood cells** are a key element of the lymphatic system which serve to prevent disease and repair the body after infection to prevent further illness.

Integumentary System

The integumentary system includes skin, hair, nails, sense receptors, sweat glands, and oil glands. The **skin** acts as a sensory organ, provides an exterior barrier against disease, regulates body temperature through perspiration, manufactures chemicals and hormones, and provides a place for nerves from the nervous system and parts of the circulation system to travel through. Skin has three layers: epidermis, dermis, and subcutaneous. The **epidermis** is the thin, outermost, waterproof layer. The **dermis** has the sweat glands, oil glands, and hair follicles. The **subcutaneous layer** has connective tissue. Also, this layer has **adipose** (i.e., fat) tissue, nerves, arteries, and veins.

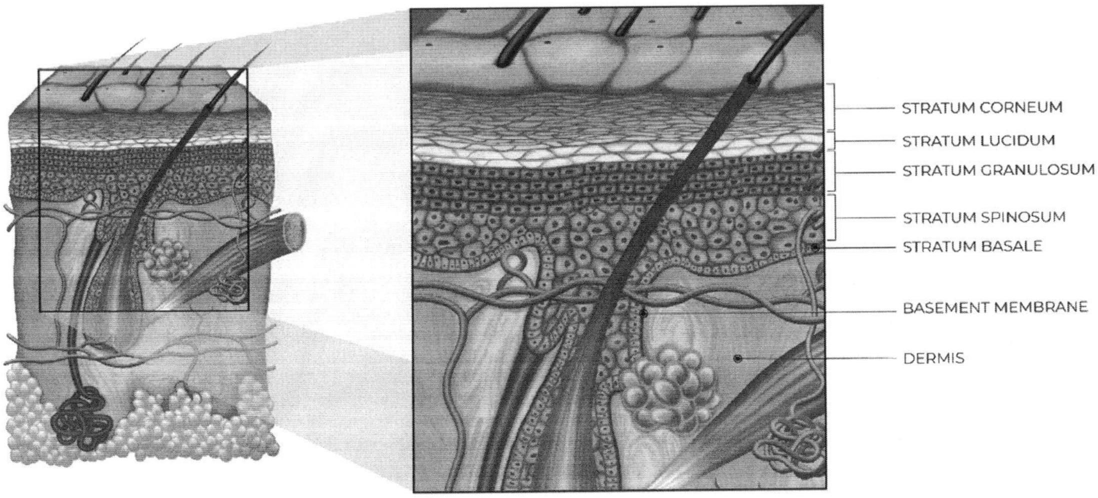

Review Video: Integumentary System
Visit mometrix.com/academy and enter code: 655980

Muscular System

The **muscular system** works in concert with the **skeletal system** to move the body and perform such core functions as cardiac activity. Key elements include:

- **Smooth muscle tissues** are involuntary muscles that are found in the walls of internal organs such as the stomach, intestines, and blood vessels. Smooth muscle tissues, or **visceral tissue,** is nonstriated. Smooth muscle cells are shorter and wider than skeletal muscle fibers. Smooth muscle tissue is also found in sphincters or valves that control the movement of material through openings throughout the body.
- **Cardiac muscle** tissue is involuntary muscle that is found only in the heart. Like skeletal muscle cells, cardiac muscle cells are also striated.
- **Skeletal muscles** are voluntary muscles that work in pairs to move parts of the skeleton. Skeletal muscles are composed of **muscle fibers** (cells) that are bound together in parallel bundles. Skeletal muscles are also known as **striated muscle** due to their striped histological appearance under a microscope.

Only skeletal muscle interacts with the skeleton to move the body. When they contract, the muscles transmit force to the attached bones. Working together, the muscles and bones act as a system of levers that move around the joints.

Review Video: Muscular System
Visit mometrix.com/academy and enter code: 967216

Major Muscles

The human body has more than 650 skeletal muscles than account for approximately half of a person's weight. Starting with the head and face, the temporalis and masseter move the mandible (lower jaw bone). The orbicularis oculi closes the eye. The orbicularis oris draws the lips together. The sternocleidomastoids move the head. The trapezius moves the shoulder, and the pectoralis major, deltoid, and latissimus dorsi move the upper arm. The biceps brachii and the triceps brachii move the lower arm. The rectus abdominis, external oblique, and erector spine move the trunk. The external and internal obliques elevate and depress the ribs. The gluteus maximus moves the upper leg. The quadriceps femoris, hamstrings, and sartorius move the lower leg. The gastrocnemius and the soleus extend the foot.

Skeletal Muscle Contraction

Skeletal muscles consist of numerous muscle fibers. Each muscle fiber contains a bundle of myofibrils, which are composed of multiple repeating contractile units called sarcomeres. **Myofibrils** contain two protein microfilaments: a thick filament and a thin filament. The **thick filament** is composed of the protein myosin. The **thin filament** is composed of the protein actin. The dark bands (striations) in skeletal muscles are formed when thick and thin filaments overlap. Light bands occur where the thin filament is overlapped. Skeletal muscle attraction occurs when the thin filaments slide over the thick filaments shortening the sarcomere. When an action potential (electrical signal) reaches a muscle fiber, calcium ions are released. According to the sliding filament model of muscle contraction, these calcium ions bind to the myosin and actin, which assists in the binding of the myosin heads of the thick filaments to the actin molecules of the thin filaments. Adenosine triphosphate released from glucose provides the energy necessary for the contraction.

Skeletal System

The skeletal system serves many functions including providing structural support, movement, and protection; producing blood cells; and storing substances such as fat and minerals. The **axial skeleton** transfers the weight from the upper body to the lower appendages. Bones provide attachment points for muscles. The cranium protects the brain. The vertebrae protect the spinal cord. The rib cage protects the heart and lungs. The pelvis protects the reproductive organs. **Joints** including hinge joints, ball-and-socket joints, pivot joints, ellipsoid joints, gliding joints, and saddle joints. The **red marrow** manufactures red and white blood cells. All bone marrow is red at birth, but adults have approximately one-half red bone marrow and one-half yellow bone marrow. Yellow bone marrow stores fat.

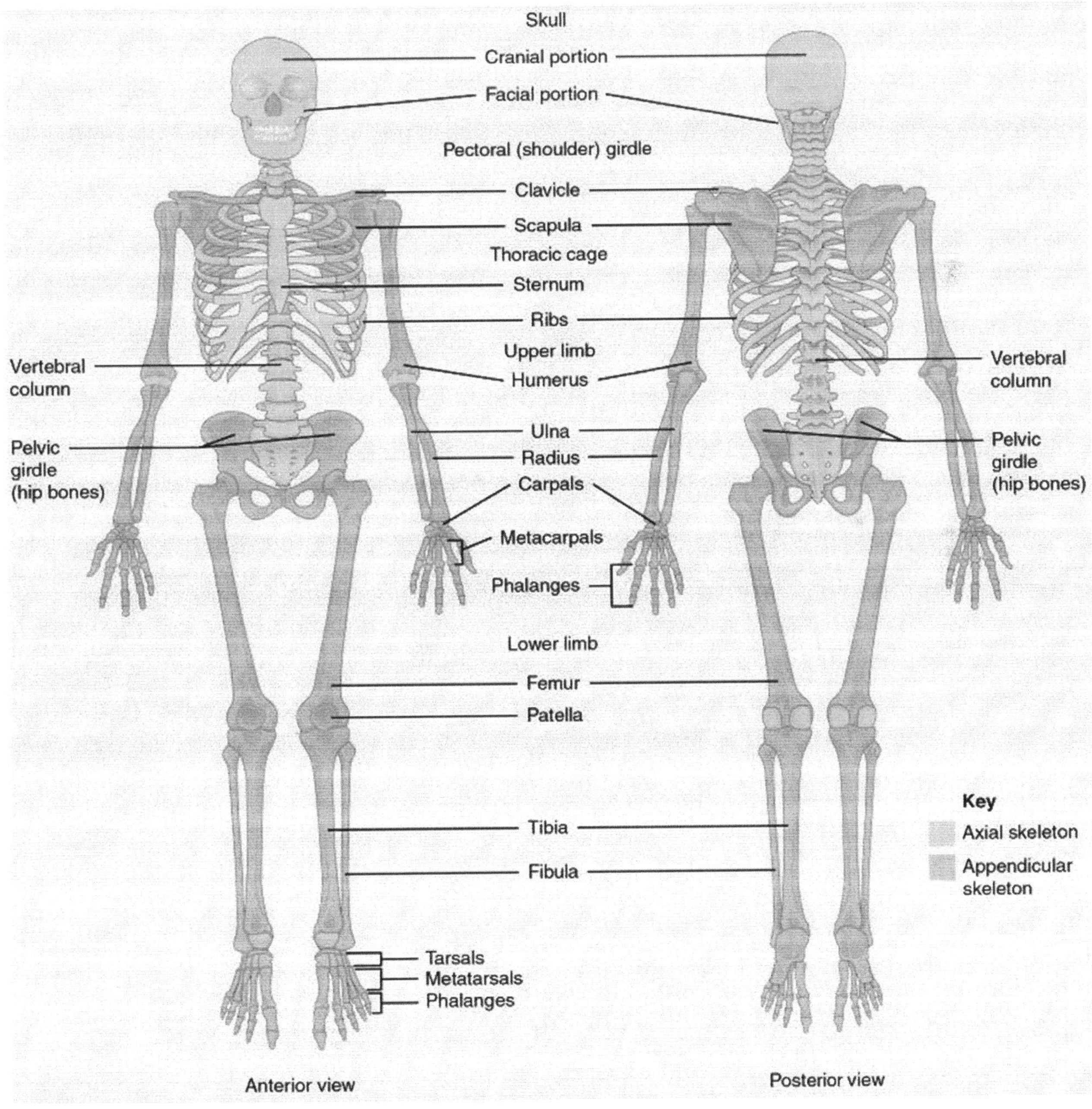

Structure of Axial Skeleton and Appendicular Skeleton

The **human skeletal system**, which consists of 206 bones along with numerous tendons, ligaments, and cartilage, is divided into the axial skeleton and the appendicular skeleton.

The **axial skeleton** consists of 80 bones and includes the vertebral column, rib cage, sternum, skull, and hyoid bone. The **vertebral column** consists of 33 vertebrae classified as cervical vertebrae, thoracic vertebrae, lumbar vertebrae, and sacral vertebrae. The **rib cage** includes 12 paired ribs, 10 pairs of true ribs and two pairs of floating ribs, and the **sternum**, which consists of the manubrium, corpus sterni, and xiphoid process. The **skull** includes the cranium and facial bones. The **ossicles** are bones in the middle ear. The **hyoid bone** provides an attachment point for the tongue muscles. The axial skeleton protects vital organs including the brain, heart, and lungs.

The **appendicular skeleton** consists of 126 bones including the pectoral girdle, pelvic girdle, and appendages. The **pectoral girdle** consists of the scapulae (shoulder blades) and clavicles (collarbones). The **pelvic girdle** attaches to the sacrum at the sacroiliac joint. The upper appendages (arms) include the humerus, radius, ulna, carpals, metacarpals, and phalanges. The lower appendages (legs) include the femur, patella, fibula, tibia, tarsals, metatarsals, and phalanges.

The axial skeleton and the appendicular skeleton:

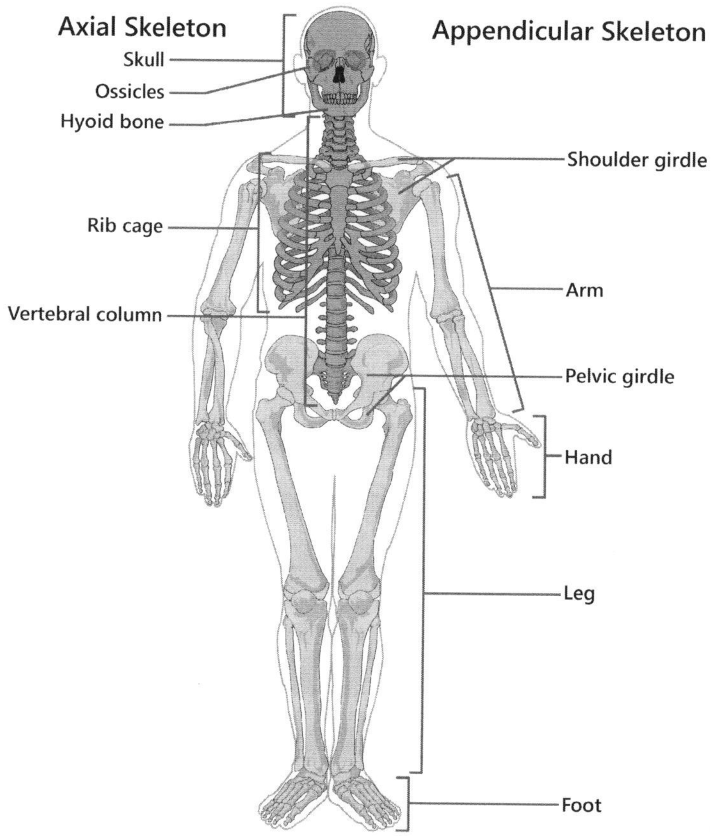

Review Video: Skeletal System
Visit mometrix.com/academy and enter code: 256447

NERVOUS SYSTEM

The human **nervous system** consists of the **central nervous system** (i.e., brain and spinal cord) and the **peripheral nervous system** (i.e., nerves). They deliver voluntary and involuntary messages throughout the body. Core functions, such as digestion and respiration, are controlled by the brain via messages sent through the peripheral nervous system. The brain also receives external cues to regulate temperature and activate certain muscle groups.

Review Video: Function of the Nervous System
Visit mometrix.com/academy and enter code: 708428

The human nervous system senses, interprets, and issues commands as a response to conditions in the body's environment. This process is made possible by a complex communication system of cells called **neurons**.

Messages are sent across the plasma membrane of neurons through a process called **action potential**. These messages occur when a neuron is stimulated past a necessary threshold. These stimulations occur in a sequence from the stimulation point of one neuron to its contact with another neuron. At the point of contact, called a **chemical synapse**, a substance is released that stimulates or inhibits the action of the adjoining cell. A network of nerves composed of neurons fans out across the body and forms the framework for the nervous system. The direction the information flows depends on the specific organizations of nerve circuits and pathways.

Review Video: What is the Function of the Nervous System
Visit mometrix.com/academy and enter code: 708428

THE SOMATIC NERVOUS SYSTEM AND THE REFLEX ARC

The somatic nervous system (**SNS**) controls the five senses and the voluntary movement of skeletal muscle. So, this system has all of the neurons that are connected to sense organs. Efferent (motor) and afferent (sensory) nerves help the somatic nervous system operate the senses and the movement of skeletal muscle. **Efferent nerves** bring signals from the central nervous system to the sensory organs and the muscles. **Afferent nerves** bring signals from the sensory organs and the muscles to the central nervous system. The somatic nervous system also performs involuntary movements which are known as reflex arcs.

A **reflex**, the simplest act of the nervous system, is an automatic response without any conscious thought to a stimulus via the reflex arc. The **reflex arc** is the simplest nerve pathway, which bypasses the brain and is controlled by the spinal cord. For example, in the classic knee-jerk response (patellar tendon reflex), the stimulus is the reflex hammer hitting the tendon, and the response is the muscle contracting, which jerks the foot upward. The stimulus is detected by sensory receptors, and a message is sent along a **sensory** (afferent) neuron to one or more

interneurons in the spinal cord. The interneuron(s) transmit this message to a **motor** (efferent) neuron, which carries the message to the correct **effector** (muscle).

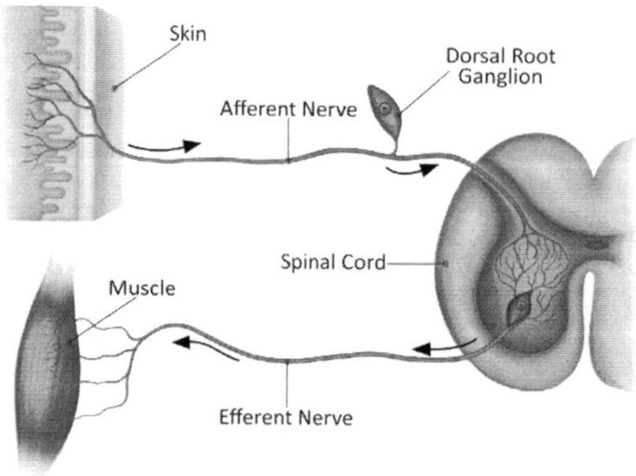

The Eyes

The eyes are a sensory organ, and therefore, belong to the nervous system. The main **parts of the eye** and their functions are as follows:

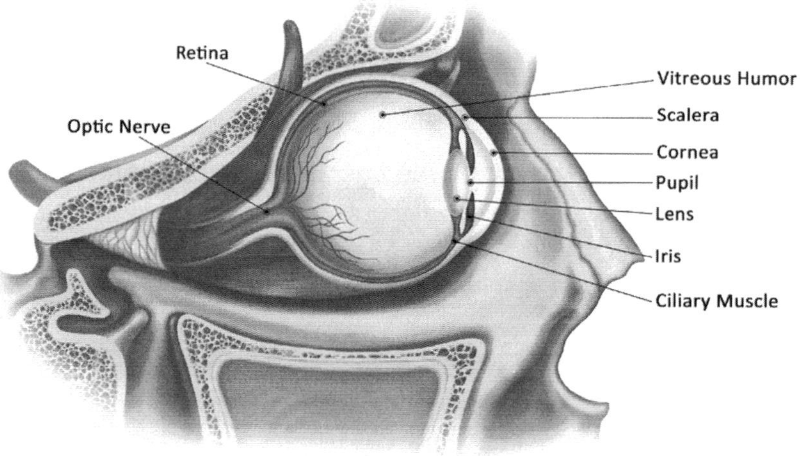

- **Aqueous humor** is watery fluid that maintains eye pressure.
- The **bony orbit** is the socket protecting the eye.
- **Cranial nerves** that help with the function of the eye such as movement or vision include:
    - the optic nerve (cranial nerve II)
    - oculomotor (III)
    - trochlear (IV)
    - trigeminal (V)
    - abducens (VI)
    - vagus (X) nerves
- **Eyelashes and lids** protect the eye and sweep out particles.
- **Extrinsic muscles** focus the eye.
- The **lacrimal glands** are tear ducts to moisten the eye.
- The **lens** refracts light.
- The **optic disc** is the blind spot.
- The **pupil** regulates light entry.
- The **retina** has rods for black and white imaging and cones for color imaging, and helps trigger the optic nerve to send impulses to the brain.
- The **macula** is at the retinal center that is very sensitive to light. The black spot in the center is called the fovea which provides the sharpest vision.
- The **choroid** is a black layer behind the retina that absorbs light and nourishes the retina.
- The **cornea** is the window at the front of the eye that helps with focus.
- The **iris** regulates light entry.
- The **sclera** is tough, white fibrous connective tissue holding nerves and vessels that acts as protection for the eye.
- The **suspensory ligament** connects the lens to the ciliary muscles of the iris.
- The **vitreous humor** is jelly that maintains the eye's shape and refracts images.

Reproductive System

The **reproductive system** consists of the prostate, testicle, penis, and scrotum in males and ovaries, uterus, vagina, fallopian tubes, and mammary glands in females. The primary function is the creation of human life. **Sperm** is produced by the testes and is delivered to the ovary-produced **eggs** in the fallopian tubes for fertilization. The uterus then serves as the home for the developing fetus. **Mammary glands** secrete nutrients for the newborn child.

Male Reproductive System

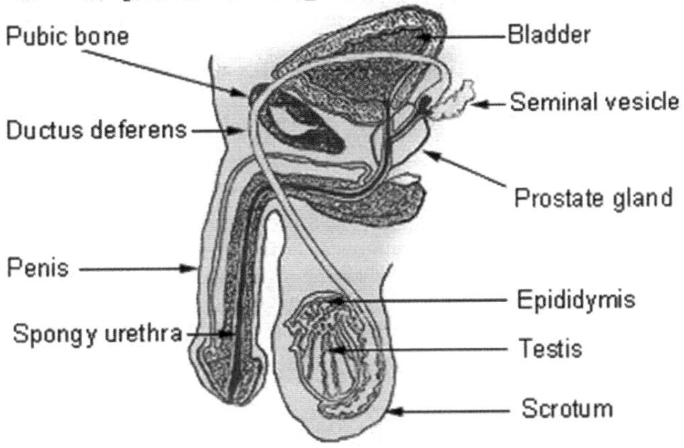

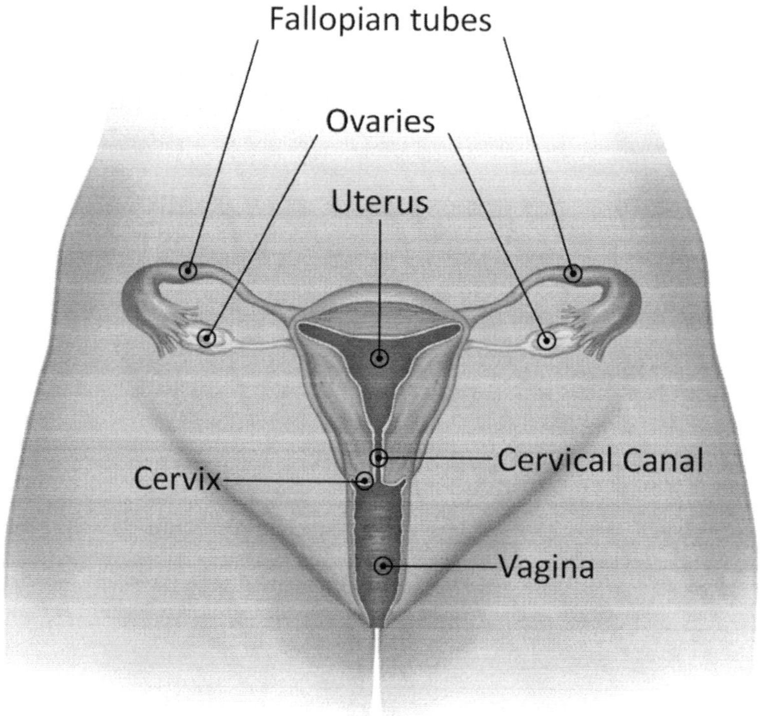

> **Review Video: Reproductive Systems**
> Visit mometrix.com/academy and enter code: 505450

Interconnectedness of Body Systems

Respiratory and Circulatory Systems Working Together

Body systems work in concert with each other to respond to increasing and decreasing demands on the body and regulate **homeostasis**, the manner in which the human body regulates itself based on internal and external conditions in order to maintain a physiological balance. For example, the heart pumps blood through the **circulatory system** to distribute oxygenated blood throughout the body to meet physiological demands at any given time. Blood becomes oxygenated in the lungs (**respiratory system**) after excess **carbon dioxide** is released from the body through respiration. Inspiration of **oxygen** into the lungs allows the blood to become oxygen-rich so as to be distributed throughout the body. When physiological demands of the body increase (i.e., quickly climbing stairs), inspiration of oxygen increases and the heart pumps faster in order to more efficiently increase the delivery of oxygenated blood throughout the body. When the intense physical activity subsides, breathing slows and the heart returns to a normal resting heart rate.

Impact of Diet and Exercise on the Circulatory System

The delivery of **oxygenated blood** throughout the body can be accomplished more efficiently with a pattern of consistent exercise and good dietary habits. **Aerobic** activity strengthens the heart by increasing the oxygen carrying capacity of the red blood cells (**hemoglobin**) while also lowering resting blood pressure. In addition, aerobic exercise helps increase high density lipoproteins (HDL) (i.e., "good cholesterol") and decreasing low density lipoproteins (i.e., "bad cholesterol") which helps keep the arteries (**circulatory system**) clear. Consistent and adequate physical activity also helps regulate blood sugars, which can reduce the likelihood of developing Type II diabetes. A high fiber, low fat diet also directly contributes to lower blood sugar levels, cholesterol management, and helps maintain healthy bowels (**digestive system**). Combining regular aerobic physical activity with a high fiber, low fat diet is one of the most effective methods to improve one's cardiovascular health, maintain a healthy weight, and increase personal longevity.

Homeostasis

Maintenance of Homeostasis in Organisms

Role of Feedback Mechanisms

Homeostasis is the regulation of internal chemistry to maintain a constant internal environment. This state is controlled through various feedback mechanisms that consist of receptors, an integrator, and effectors. **Receptors** such as mechanoreceptors or thermoreceptors in the skin detect the stimuli. Then, an **integrator**, such as the brain or spinal cord, receives the information concerning the stimuli and sends out signals to other parts of the body. Finally, **effectors**, such as muscles or glands, respond to the stimulus. Basically, the receptors receive the stimuli and notify an integrator, which signals the effectors to respond.

Feedback mechanisms can be negative or positive. **Negative-feedback** mechanisms are mechanisms that provide a decrease in response with an increase in stimulus that inhibits the stimulus, which in turn decreases the response. **Positive-feedback** mechanisms are mechanisms that provide an increase in response with an increase in stimulus, which actually increases the stimulus, which in turn increases the response.

Role of Hypothalamus

The hypothalamus plays a major role in the homoeostasis of vertebrates. The **hypothalamus** is the central portion of the brain just above the brainstem and is linked to the endocrine system through the pituitary gland. The hypothalamus releases special hormones that influence the secretion of pituitary hormones. The hypothalamus regulates the fundamental physiological state by controlling body temperature, hunger, thirst, sleep, behaviors related to attachment, sexual development, fight-or-flight stress response, and circadian rhythms.

Role of Endocrine System and Hormones

All vertebrates have an **endocrine system** that consists of numerous ductless glands that produce hormones to help coordinate many functions of the body. **Hormones** are signaling molecules that are received by receptors. Many hormones are secreted in response to signals from the pituitary gland and hypothalamus gland. Other hormones are secreted in response to signals from inside the body. Hormones can consist of amino acids, proteins, or lipid molecules such as steroid hormones. Hormones can affect target cells, which have the correct receptor that is able to bind to that particular hormone. Most cells have receptors for more than one type of hormone. Hormones are distributed to the target cells in the blood by the cardiovascular system. Hormones incorporate feedback mechanisms to help the body maintain homeostasis.

Role of Antidiuretic Hormone

Antidiuretic hormone (ADH) helps maintain homeostasis in vertebrates. ADH is produced by the posterior pituitary gland, and it regulates the reabsorption of water in the kidneys and concentrates the urine. The stimulus in this feedback mechanism is a drop in blood volume due to water loss. This signal is picked up by the hypothalamus, which signals the pituitary gland to secrete ADH. ADH is carried by the cardiovascular system to the nephrons in the kidneys signaling them to reabsorb more water and send less out as waste. As more water is reabsorbed, the blood volume increases, which is monitored by the hypothalamus. As the blood volume reaches the set point, the hypothalamus signals for a decrease in the secretion of ADH, and the cycle continues.

Role of Insulin and Glucagon

Insulin and glucagon are hormones that help maintain the glucose concentration in the blood. Insulin and glucagon are secreted by the clumps of endocrine cells called the **pancreatic islets** that are located in the pancreas. Insulin and glucagon work together to maintain the blood glucose level. **Insulin** stimulates cells to remove glucose from the blood. **Glucagon** stimulates the liver to convert glycogen to glucose. After eating, glucose levels increase in the blood. This stimulus signals the pancreas to stop the secretion of glucagon and to start secreting insulin. Cells respond to the insulin and remove glucose from the blood, lowering the level of glucose in the blood. Later, after eating, the level of glucose in the blood decreases further. This stimulus signals the pancreas to secrete glucagon and decrease the secretion of insulin. In response to the stimulus, the liver converts glycogen to glucose, and the level of glucose in the blood rises. When the individual eats, the cycle begins again.

Thermoregulation

Animals exhibit many adaptations that help them achieve homeostasis, or a stable internal environment. Some of these adaptions are behavioral. Most organisms exhibit some type of behavioral thermoregulation. **Thermoregulation** is the ability to keep the body temperature within certain boundaries. The type of behavioral thermoregulation depends on whether the animal is an ectotherm or an endotherm. **Ectotherms** are "cold-blooded," and their body temperature changes with their external environment. **Endotherms** are "warm-blooded" and maintain a stable body temperature by internal means.

To regulate their temperature, ectotherms often move to an appropriate location. For example, fish move to warmer waters while animals will climb to higher grounds. **Diurnal ectotherms** such as reptiles often bask in the sun to increase their body temperatures. Butterflies are special ectotherms classified as **heliotherms** since they get nearly all of their heat from basking in the sun.

While they have internal systems that regulate temperature, many endotherms that live in hot environments have adapted to the nocturnal lifestyle. Desert animals are often nocturnal to escape high daytime temperatures. Other nocturnal animals sleep during the day in underground burrows or dens.

Reproduction, Development, and Growth in Animals

Gamete Formation

Gametogenesis is the formation of gametes, or reproductive cells. Gametes are produced by meiosis. **Meiosis** is a special type of cell division that consists of two consecutive mitotic divisions referred to as meiosis I and meiosis II. **Meiosis I** is a reduction division in which a diploid cell is reduced to two haploid daughter cells that contain only one of each pair of homologous chromosomes. During **meiosis II**, those haploid cells are further divided to form four haploid cells. **Spermatogenesis** in males produces four viable sperm cells from each complete cycle of meiosis. **Oogenesis** produces four daughter cells, but only one is a viable egg and the other three are polar bodies.

Fertilization

Fertilization is the union of a sperm cell and an egg cell to produce a zygote. Many sperm may bind to an egg, but only one joins with the egg and injects its nuclei into the egg. Fertilization can be external or internal. **External fertilization** takes place outside of the female's body. For example, many fish, amphibians, crustaceans, mollusks, and corals reproduce externally by **spawning** or releasing gametes into the water simultaneously or right after each other. Reptiles and birds reproduce by **internal fertilization**. All mammals except monotremes (e.g. platypus) reproduce by internal fertilization.

Embryonic Development

Embryonic development in animals is typically divided into four stages: cleavage, patterning, differentiation, and growth. **Cleavage** occurs immediately after fertilization when the large single-celled zygote immediately begins to divide into smaller and smaller cells without an increase in mass. A hollow ball of cells forms a blastula. Next, during patterning, gastrulation occurs. During gastrulation, the cells are organized into three primary germ layers: ectoderm, mesoderm, and endoderm. Then, the cells in these layers differentiate into special tissues and organs. For example, the nervous system develops from the ectoderm. The muscular system develops from the mesoderm. Much of the digestive system develops from the endoderm. The final stage of embryonic development is growth and further tissue specialization. The embryo continues to grow until ready for hatching or birth.

Postnatal Growth

Postnatal growth occurs from hatching or birth until death. The length of the postnatal growth depends on the species. Elephants can live 70 years, but mice only about 4 years. Right after animals are hatched or born, they go through a period of rapid growth and development. In vertebrates, bones lengthen, muscles grow in bulk, and fat is deposited. At maturity, bones stop growing in length, but bones can grow in width and repair themselves throughout the animal's lifetime, and muscle deposition slows down. Fat cells continue to increase and decrease in size throughout the animal's life. Growth is controlled by genetics but is also influenced by nutrition and disease. Most animals are sexually mature in less than two years and can produce offspring.

Characteristics of Major Plant Divisions

Vascular and Nonvascular Plants

Vascular plants, also referred to as **tracheophytes**, have dermal tissue, meristematic tissue, ground tissues, and vascular tissues. Nonvascular plants, also referred to as **bryophytes**, do not have the vascular tissue xylem and phloem. Vascular plants can grow very tall, whereas nonvascular plants are short and close to the ground. Vascular plants can be found in dry regions, but nonvascular plants typically grow near or in moist areas. Vascular plants have leaves, roots, and stems, but nonvascular plants have leaf-like, root-like, and stem-like structures that do not have true vascular tissue. Nonvascular plants have hair-like **rhizoids**, that act like roots by anchoring them to the ground and absorbing water. Vascular plants include angiosperms, gymnosperms, and ferns. Nonvascular plants include mosses and liverworts.

Flowering Versus Nonflowering Plants

Angiosperms and gymnosperms are both vascular plants. **Angiosperms** are flowering plants, and **gymnosperms** are non-flowering plants. Angiosperms reproduce by seeds that are enclosed in an ovary, usually in a fruit, while gymnosperms reproduce by unenclosed or "naked" seeds on scales, leaves, or cones. Angiosperms can be further classified as either monocots or dicots, depending on if they have one or two cotyledons, respectively. Angiosperms include grasses, garden flowers, vegetables, and broadleaf trees such as maples, birches, elms, and oaks. Gymnosperms include conifers such as pines, spruces, cedars, and redwoods.

Review Video: Kingdom Plantae Characteristics
Visit mometrix.com/academy and enter code: 710084

Monocots and Dicots

Angiosperms can be classified as either monocots or dicots. The seeds of **monocots** have one cotyledon, and the seeds of **dicots** have two cotyledons. The flowers of monocots have petals in multiples of three, and the flowers of dicots have petals in multiples of four or five. The leaves of monocots are slender with parallel veins, while the leaves of dicots are broad and flat with branching veins. The vascular bundles in monocots are distributed throughout the stem, whereas the vascular bundles in dicots are arranged in rings. Monocots have a **fibrous root system**, and dicots have a **taproot system**.

Major Plant Tissues and Organs

Plant Dermal Tissue

Plant dermal tissue is called the epidermis, and is usually a single layer of closely-packed cells that covers leaves and young stems. The epidermis protects the plant by secreting the cuticle, which is a waxy substance that helps prevent water loss and infections. The epidermis in leaves has tiny pores called **stomata**. Guard cells in the epidermis control the opening and closing of the stomata. The epidermis usually does not have chloroplasts. The epidermis may be replaced by periderm in older plants. The **periderm** is also referred to as bark. The layers of the periderm are cork cells or phellem, phelloderm, and cork cambium or phellogen. Cork is the outer layer of the periderm and consists of nonliving cells. The periderm protects the plant and provides insulation.

Plant Vascular Tissue

The two major types of plant vascular tissue are xylem and phloem. Xylem and phloem are bound together in vascular bundles. A meristem called vascular cambium is located between the xylem and phloem and produces new xylem and phloem. **Xylem** is made up of tracheids and vessel elements. All vascular plants contain tracheids, but only angiosperms contain vessel elements. Xylem provides support and transports water and dissolved minerals unidirectionally from the roots upward using processes like transpiration pull and root pressure. Phloem is made up of companion cells and sieve-tube cells. **Phloem** transports dissolved sugars produced during photosynthesis and other nutrients bidirectionally to non-photosynthetic areas of the plant. By active transport, the companion vessels move glucose in and out of the sieve-tube cells.

Plant Ground Tissue

The three major types of ground tissue are parenchyma tissue, collenchyma tissue, and sclerenchyma tissue. Most ground tissue is made up of parenchyma. **Parenchyma** is formed by parenchyma cells, and it function in photosynthesis, food storage, and tissue repair. The inner tissue of a leaf, mesophyll, is an example of parenchyma tissue. **Collenchyma** is made of collenchyma cells and provides support in roots, stems, and petioles. **Sclerenchyma** tissue is made of sclereid cells, which are more rigid than the collenchyma cells, and provides rigid support and protection. Plant sclerenchyma tissue may contain cellulose or lignin. Fabrics such as jute, hemp, and flax are made of sclerenchyma tissue.

Plant Meristematic Tissue

Meristems or meristematic tissues are regions of plant growth. The cells in meristems are undifferentiated and always remain **totipotent**, which means they can always develop into any type of special tissue. Meristem cells can divide and produce new cells, which can aid in the process of regenerating damaged parts. Cells of meristems reproduce asexually through mitosis or cell division that is regulated by hormones. The two types of meristems are lateral meristems and apical meristems. **Primary growth** occurs at **apical meristems**, located at the tip of roots and shoots, and increases the length of the plant. Primary meristems include the protoderm, which produces epidermis; the procambium, which produces cambium, or lateral meristems; xylem and phloem; and the ground meristem, which produces ground tissue including parenchyma. **Secondary growth** occurs at the lateral or secondary meristems and causes an increase in diameter or thickness.

Flowers

The primary function of flowers is to produce seeds for reproduction of the plant. Flowers have a **pedicel**, a stalk with a receptacle or enlarged upper portion, which holds the developing seeds. Flowers also can have sepals and petals. **Sepals** are leaflike structures that protect the bud. **Petals**, which are collectively called the corolla, help to attract pollinators. Plants can have stamens, pistils, or both depending on the type of plant. The **stamen** consists of the anther and filament. The end of the stamen is called the **anther** and is where pollen is produced. Pollen also contains sperm, which is needed in order for a proper plant zygot to form. The **pistil** consists of the stigma, style, and ovary. The ovary contains the ovules, which house the egg cells.

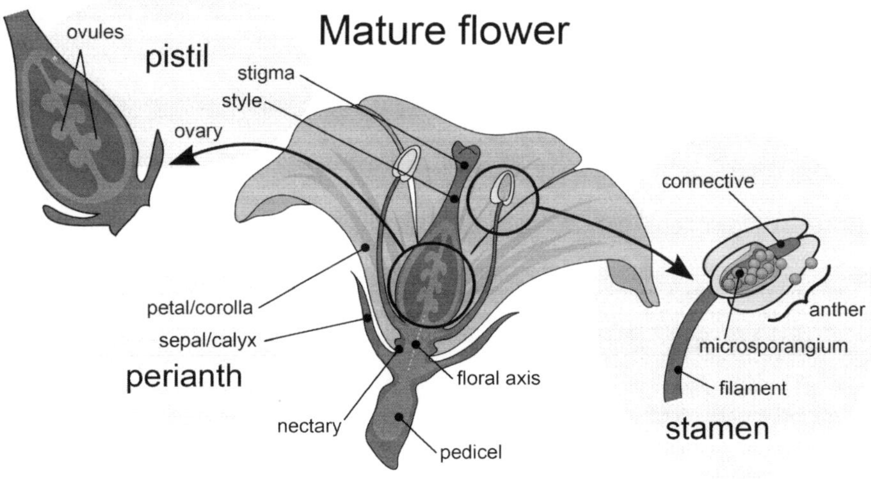

Stems

Plants can have either woody or nonwoody (herbaceous) stems. **Woody** stems consist of wood, or bark, as a structural tissue, while **herbaceous** stems are very flexible. The stem is divided into nodes and internodes. Buds are located at the nodes and may develop into leaves, roots, flowers, cones, or more stems. Stems consist of dermal tissue, ground tissue, and vascular tissue. **Monocot stems have vascular bundles distributed through the stem. Dicots have rings of vascular bundles**. Stems have four main functions: (1) they provide support to leaves, flowers, and fruits;

(2) they transport materials in the xylem and phloem; (3) they store food; and (4) they have meristems, which provide all of the new cells for the plant.

MONOCOT		DICOT	
Single Cotyledon		Two Cotyledon	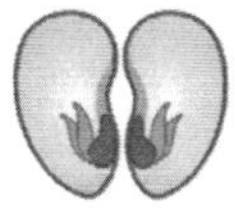
Long Narrow Leaf Parallel Veins		Broad Leaf Network of Veins	
Vascular Bundles Scattered	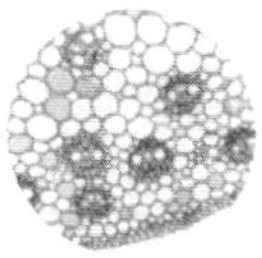	Vascular Bundles in a Ring	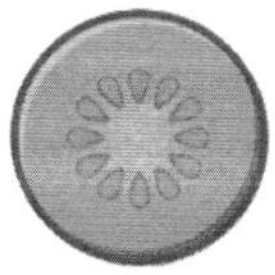
Floral Parts in Multiples of 3		Floral Parts in Multiples of 4 or 5	

LEAVES

The primary function of a **leaf** is to manufacture food through photosynthesis. The leaf consists of a flat portion called the **blade** and a stalk called the **petiole**. The edge of the leaf is called the margin and can be entire, toothed, or lobed. Veins transport food and water and make up the skeleton of the leaf. The large central vein is called the **midrib**. The blade has an upper and lower epidermis. The epidermis is covered by a protective cuticle. The lower epidermis contains many stomata, which are pores that allow air to enter and leave the leaf. Stomata also regulate transpiration. The middle portion of the leaf is called the **mesophyll**. The mesophyll consists of the palisade mesophyll and the spongy mesophyll. Most photosynthesis occurs in chloroplasts located in the palisade mesophyll.

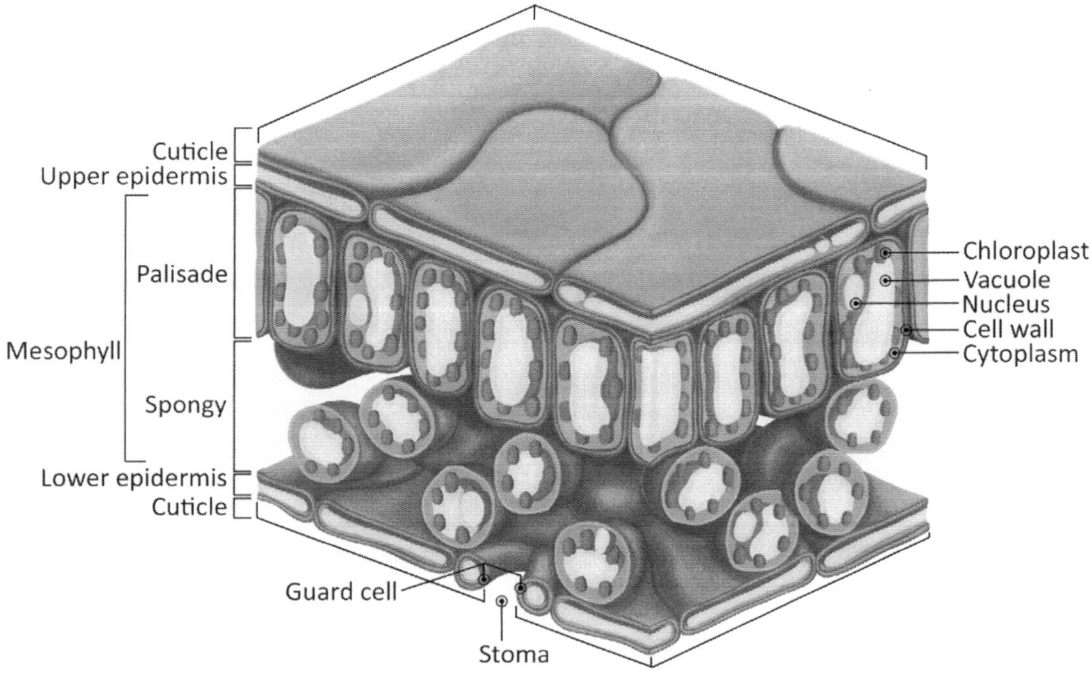

Roots

The primary functions of roots are to anchor the plant, absorb materials, and store food. The two basic types of root systems are taproot systems and fibrous root systems. **Taproot systems** have a primary root with many smaller secondary roots. **Fibrous root systems**, which lack a primary root, consist of a mass of many small secondary roots. The root has three main regions: the area of maturation, the area of elongation, and the area of cell division or the meristematic region. The root is covered by an epidermal cell, some of which develops into root hairs. **Root hairs** absorb water and minerals by osmosis, and capillary action helps move the water upward through the roots to the rest of the plant. The center of the root is the **vascular cylinder**, which contains the xylem and phloem. The vascular cylinder is surrounded by the cortex where the food is stored. Primary growth occurs at the root tip. Secondary growth occurs at the vascular cambium located between the xylem and phloem.

Plant Life Cycles and Reproductive Strategies

Pollination Strategies

Pollination is the transfer of pollen from the anther of the stamen to the stigma of the pistil on the same plant or on a different plant. Pollinators can be either **abiotic** (not derived from a living organism) or **biotic** (derived from a living organism). Abiotic pollinators include wind and water. Approximately 20% of pollination occurs by abiotic pollinators. For example, grasses are typically pollinated by wind, and aquatic plants are typically pollinated by water. Biotic pollinators include insects, birds, mammals, and occasionally reptiles. Most biotic pollinators are insects. Many plants have colored petals and strong scents, which attract insects. Pollen rubs off on the insects and is transferred as they move from plant to plant.

Seed Dispersal Methods

Methods of **seed dispersal** can be abiotic or biotic. Methods of seed dispersal include gravity, wind, water, and animals. Some plants produce seeds in fruits that get eaten by animals and then are distributed to new locations in the animals' waste. Some seeds (e.g. dandelions) have structures to aid in dispersal by wind. Some seeds have barbs that get caught in animal hair or bird feathers and are then carried to new locations by the animals. Interestingly, some animals bury seeds for food storage but do not return for the seeds. The seeds of aquatic plants can be dispersed by water, while the seeds of plants near rivers, streams, lakes, and beaches (e.g. coconuts) are also often dispersed by water. Some plants, in a method called **mechanical dispersal**, can propel or shoot their seeds away from them even up to several feet. For example, touch-me-nots and violets utilize mechanical dispersal.

Alternation of Generations

Alternation of generations, also referred to as **metagenesis**, contains both a sexual phase and an asexual phase in the life cycle of the plant. Mosses and ferns reproduce by alternation of generations: the sexual phase is called the **gametophyte**, and the asexual phase is called the **sporophyte**. During the sexual phase, a sperm fertilizes an egg to form a zygote. By mitosis, the zygote develops into the sporophyte. The sporangia in the sori of the sporophyte produce the spores through meiosis. The spores germinate and by mitosis produce the gametophyte.

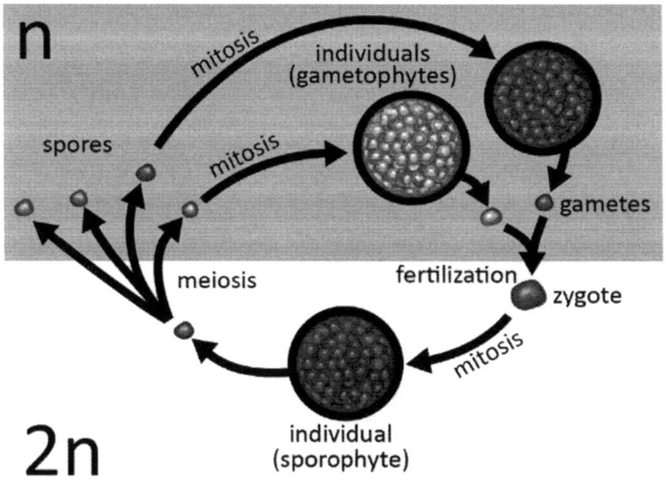

Plant Transportation of Water and Nutrients

Obtaining and Transporting Water and Inorganic Nutrients

Inorganic nutrients and water enter plants through the root hair and travel to the xylem. Once the water, minerals, and salts have crossed the endodermis, they must be moved upward through the xylem by water uptake. Most of a plant's water is lost through the stomata by transpiration. This loss is necessary to provide the tension needed to pull the water and nutrients up through the xylem. In order to maintain the remaining water that is necessary for the functioning of the plant, guard cells control the stomata. Whether an individual stoma is closed or open is controlled by two guard cells. When the guard cells lose water and become flaccid, they collapse together, closing the stoma. When the guard cells swell with water and become turgid, they move apart, opening the stoma.

Use of Roots

Plant roots have numerous root hairs that absorb water and inorganic nutrients such as minerals and salts. Root hairs are thin, hair-like outgrowths of the root's epidermal cells that exponentially increase the root's surface area. Water molecules cross the cell membranes of the root hairs by **osmosis** and then travel on to the vascular cylinder. Inorganic nutrients are transported across the cell membranes of the root endodermis by **active transport**. The endodermis is a single layer of cells that the water and nutrients must pass through by osmosis or active transport. To control mineral uptake by the roots, Casparian strips act as an extracellular diffusion barrier, and forces nutrients to be pulled into the plant. While water passes through by osmosis, mineral uptake is controlled by transport proteins.

Use of Xylem

The xylem contains dead, water-conducting cells called tracheids and vessels. The movement of water upward through the tracheids and vessels is explained by the **cohesion-tension theory**. First, water is lost through evaporation of the plant's surface through transpiration. This can occur at any surface exposed to air but is mainly through the stomata in the epidermis. This transpiration puts the water inside the xylem in a state of tension. Because water is cohesive due to the strong hydrogen bonds between molecules, the water is pulled up the xylem as long as the water is transpiring.

Products of Photosynthesis

Glucose Produced During Photosynthesis

Plants produce glucose, a simple carbohydrate or monosaccharide, during photosynthesis. Plants do not transport glucose molecules directly, but instead glucose undergoes reactions to form sucrose, starch, and cellulose which are then used in different ways. Glucose is joined to a fructose molecule to form **sucrose**, a disaccharide, which is transported in sap. Like glucose, sucrose is also considered a simple carbohydrate. Starches and cellulose are complex carbohydrates consisting of long chains of glucose molecules called polysaccharides. Plants use **starch** to store glucose, and **cellulose** for rigidity in cell walls.

Use of Phloem to Transport Products of Photosynthesis

The movement of sugars and other materials from the leaves to other tissues throughout the plants is called **translocation**. Nutrients are translocated from **sources**, or areas with excess sugars such as mature leaves, to **sinks**, areas where sugars are needed (i.e. roots or developing seeds). Phloem vessels are found in the vascular bundles along with the xylem. Phloem contains conducting cells called sieve elements, which are connected end to end in sieve tubes. **Sieve tubes** carry sap from sugar sources to sugar sinks. Phloem sap contains mostly sucrose dissolved in water. The sap can also contain proteins, amino acids, and hormones. Some plants transport sugar alcohols. Loading the sugar into the sieve tubes causes water to enter the tubes by osmosis, creating a higher hydrostatic pressure at the source end of the tube. This pressure is what causes nutrients to move upward towards the sink areas. Sugar is removed from the sieve tube at the sink end and the solute potential is increased, thus causing water to leave the phloem. This process is referred to as the **pressure-flow mechanism**.

Chapter Quiz

Ready to see how well you retained what you just read? Scan the QR code to go directly to the chapter quiz interface for this study guide. If you're using a computer, simply visit the online resources page at **mometrix.com/resources719/ssreglivingenv** and click the Chapter Quizzes link.

Genetics

Mendel's Laws

Law of Segregation

The **law of segregation** states that the alleles for a trait separate when gametes are formed, which means that only one of the pair of alleles for a given trait is passed to the gamete. This can be shown in monohybrid crosses, which can be used to show which allele is **dominant** for a single trait. A **monohybrid cross** is a genetic cross between two organisms with a different variation for a single trait. The first monohybrid cross typically occurs between two **homozygous** parents. Each parent is homozygous for a separate allele (gg or GG) for a particular trait. For example, in pea plants, green seeds (G) are dominant over yellow seeds (g). Therefore, in a genetic cross of two pea plants that are homozygous for seed color, the F_1 generation will be 100% **heterozygous** green seeds.

	g	**g**
G	Gg	Gg
G	Gg	Gg

Review Video: Punnett Square
Visit mometrix.com/academy and enter code: 853855

Monohybrid Cross for a Cross Between Two Gg Parents

If the plants with the heterozygous green seeds are crossed, the F_1 generation should be 50% heterozygous green (Gg), 25% homozygous green (GG), and 25% homozygous yellow (gg).

	G	**g**
G	GG	Gg
g	Gg	gg

Law of Independent Assortment

Mendel's law of independent assortment states that alleles of one characteristic or trait separate independently of the alleles of another characteristic. Therefore, the allele a gamete receives for one gene does not influence the allele received for another gene due to the allele pairs separating independently during gamete formation. This means that traits are transmitted independently of each other. This can be shown in dihybrid crosses.

Gene, Genotype, Phenotype, and Allele

A **gene** is a portion of DNA that identifies how traits are expressed and passed on in an organism. A gene is part of the genetic code. Collectively, all genes form the **genotype** of an individual. The genotype includes genes that may not be expressed, such as recessive genes. The **phenotype** is the physical, visual manifestation of genes. It is determined by the basic genetic information and how genes have been affected by their environment.

An **allele** is a variation of a gene. Also known as a trait, it determines the manifestation of a gene. This manifestation results in a specific physical appearance of some facet of an organism, such as eye color or height. The genetic information for eye color is a gene. The gene variations responsible for blue, green, brown, or black eyes are called alleles. **Locus** (plural, *loci*) refers to the location of a gene or alleles.

Review Video: Genotype vs Phenotype
Visit mometrix.com/academy and enter code: 922853

Dominant and Recessive Genes

Gene traits are represented in pairs with an uppercase letter for the **dominant trait** (A) and a lowercase letter for the **recessive trait** (a). Genes occur in pairs (AA, Aa, or aa). There is one gene on each chromosome half supplied by each parent organism. Since half the genetic material is from each parent, the offspring's traits are represented as a combination of these. A dominant trait only requires one gene of a gene pair for it to be expressed in a phenotype, whereas a recessive requires both genes in order to be manifested. For example, if the mother's genotype is Dd and the father's is dd, the possible combinations are Dd and dd. The dominant trait will be manifested if the genotype is DD or Dd. The recessive trait will be manifested if the genotype is dd. Both DD and dd are **homozygous** pairs. Dd is **heterozygous**.

Dihybrid Cross for the F_2 Generation of a Cross between GGRR and ggrr Parents

A **dihybrid cross** is a genetic cross for two traits that each have two alleles. For example, in pea plants, green seeds (G) are dominant over yellow seeds (g), and round seeds (R) are dominant over wrinkled seeds (r). In a genetic cross of two pea plants that are homozygous for seed color and seed shape (GGRR or ggRR), the F_1 generation will be 100% heterozygous green and round seeds (GgRr). If these F_1 plants (GgRr) are crossed, the resulting F_2 generation is shown below. Out of the 16 total genotypes for the cross of green, round seeds, there are only four possible phenotypes, or physical traits of the seed: green and round seed (GGRR, GGRr, GgRR, or GgRr), green and wrinkled seed (GGrr or Ggrr), yellow and round seed (ggRR or ggRr) , or yellow and wrinkled seed (ggrr). There are nine green and round seed plants, three green and wrinkled seed plants, three yellow and round seed plants, and only one yellow and wrinkled seed plant. This cross has a **9:3:3:1 ratio**.

	GR	**gR**	**Gr**	**gr**
GR	GGRR	GgRR	GGRr	GgRr
gR	GgRR	ggRR	GgRr	ggRr
Gr	GGRr	GgRr	GGrr	Ggrr
gr	GgRr	ggRr	Ggrr	ggrr

Pedigree

Pedigree analysis is a type of genetic analysis in which an inherited trait is studied and traced through several generations of a family to determine how that trait is inherited. A **pedigree** is a chart arranged as a type of family tree using symbols for people and lines to represent the relationships between those people. Squares usually represent males, and circles represent females. Horizontal lines represent a male and female mating, and the vertical lines beneath them represent their children. Usually, family members who possess the trait are fully shaded and those who only carry the trait are half-shaded. Genotypes and phenotypes are determined for each individual if possible. The pedigree below shows the family tree of a family in which the first male who was red-green color blind mated with the first female who was unaffected. They had five children. The three sons were unaffected, and the two daughters were carriers.

Inheritance of Red-Green Color Blindness:
an X-linked Recessive Trait

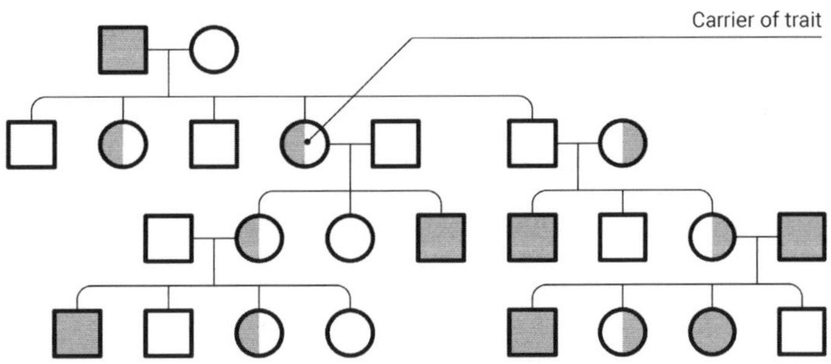

Processes Affecting the Gene Pool

Genetic Drift

Genetic drift is a microevolutionary process that causes random changes in allele frequencies that are not the result of natural selection. Genetic drift can result in a loss of genetic diversity. Genetic drift greatly impacts small populations. Two special forms of genetic drift are the genetic bottleneck and the founder effect. A **genetic bottleneck** occurs when there is a drastic reduction in population due to some change such as overhunting, disease, or habitat loss. When a population is greatly reduced in size, many alleles can be lost. Even if the population size greatly increases again, the lost alleles represent lost genetic diversity. The **founder effect** occurs when one individual or a few individuals populate a new area such as an island. This new population is limited to the alleles of the founder(s) unless mutations occur or new individuals immigrate to the region.

Gene Flow

Gene flow is a microevolutionary process in which alleles enter a population by immigration and leave a population by emigration. Gene flow helps counter genetic drift. When individuals from one genetically distinct population immigrate to a different genetically distinct population, alleles and their genetic information are added to the new population. The added alleles will change the gene frequencies within the population. This increases genetic diversity. If individuals with rare alleles emigrate from a population, the genetic diversity is decreased. Gene flow reduces the genetic differences between populations.

Chapter Quiz

Ready to see how well you retained what you just read? Scan the QR code to go directly to the chapter quiz interface for this study guide. If you're using a computer, simply visit the online resources page at **mometrix.com/resources719/ssreglivingenv** and click the Chapter Quizzes link.

Evolution

Mechanics of Evolution

Mechanisms of Evolution

Natural and Artificial Selection

Natural selection and artificial selection are both mechanisms of evolution. **Natural selection** is a process of nature in which a population can change over generations. Every population has variations in individual heritable traits and organisms best suited for survival typically reproduce and pass on those genetic traits to offspring to increase the likelihood of them surviving. Typically, the more advantageous a trait is, the more common that trait becomes in a population. Natural selection brings about evolutionary **adaptations** and is responsible for biological diversity. Artificial selection is another mechanism of evolution. **Artificial selection** is a process brought about by humans. Artificial selection is the selective breeding of domesticated animals and plants such as when farmers choose animals or plants with desirable traits to reproduce. Artificial selection has led to the evolution of farm stock and crops. For example, cauliflower, broccoli, and cabbage all evolved due to artificial selection of the wild mustard plant.

Sexual Selection

Sexual selection is a special case of natural selection in animal populations. **Sexual selection** occurs because some animals are more likely to find mates than other animals. The two main contributors to sexual selection are **competition** of males and **mate selection** by females. An example of male competition is in the mating practices of the redwing blackbird. Some males have huge territories and numerous mates that they defend. Other males have small territories, and some even have no mates. An example of mate selection by females is the mating practices of peacocks. Male peacocks display large, colorful tail feathers to attract females. Females are more likely to choose males with the larger, more colorful displays.

Coevolution

Coevolution describes a rare phenomenon in which two populations with a close ecological relationship undergo reciprocal adaptations simultaneously and evolve together, affecting each other's evolution. General examples of coevolution include predator and prey, or plant and pollinator, and parasites and their hosts. A specific example of coevolution is the yucca moths and the yucca plants. Yucca plants can only be pollinated by the yucca moths. The yucca moths lay their eggs in the yucca flowers, and their larvae grow inside the ovary.

Adaptive Radiation

Adaptive radiation is an evolutionary process in which a species branches out and adapts and fills numerous unoccupied ecological niches. The adaptations occur relatively quickly, driven by natural selection and resulting in new phenotypes and possibly new species eventually. An example of adaptive radiation is the finches that Darwin studied on the Galápagos Islands. Darwin recorded 13 different varieties of finches, which differed in the size and shape of their beaks. Through the process of natural selection, each type of finch adapted to the specific environment and specifically the food sources of the island to which it belonged. On newly formed islands with many unoccupied ecological niches, the adaptive radiation process occurred quickly due to the lack of competing species and predators.

Evidence Supporting Evolution

MOLECULAR EVIDENCE

Because all organisms are made up of cells, all organisms are alike on a fundamental level. Cells share similar components, which are made up of molecules. Specifically, all cells contain DNA and RNA. This should indicate that all species descended from a **common ancestor**. Humans and chimpanzees share approximately 98% of their genes in common, while humans and bacteria share approximately 7% of their genes in common suggesting that bacteria and humans are not closely related. Biologists have been able to use DNA sequence comparisons of modern organisms to reconstruct the "root" of the tree of life. The fact that RNA can store information, replicate itself, and code for proteins suggests that RNA could have could have evolved first, followed by DNA.

HOMOLOGY

Homology is the similarity of structures of different species based on a similar anatomy in a common evolutionary ancestor. For instance, the forelimbs of humans, dogs, birds, and whales all have the same basic pattern of the bones. Specifically, all of these organisms have a humerus, radius, and ulna. They are all modifications of the same basic evolutionary structure from a common ancestor. Tetrapods resemble the fossils of extinct transitional animal called the *Eusthenopteron*. This would seem to indicate that evolution primarily modifies preexisting structures.

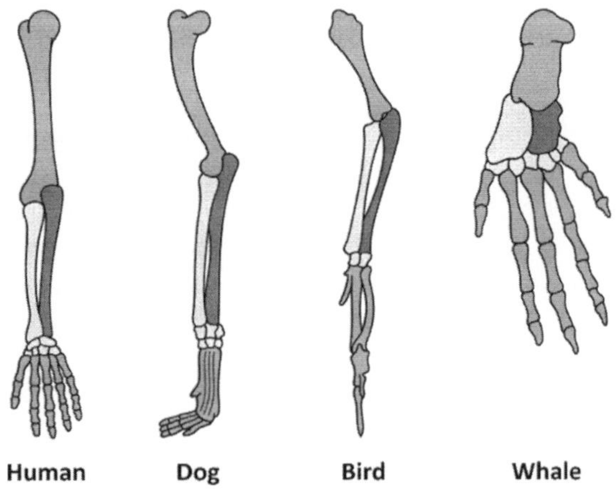

Review Video: Homologous vs Analogous Structures
Visit mometrix.com/academy and enter code: 355157

EMBRYOLOGY

The stages of **embryonic development** reveal homologies between species. These homologies are evidence of a **common ancestor**. For example, in chicken embryos and mammalian embryos, both include a stage in which slits and arches appear in the embryo's neck region that are strikingly similar to gill slits and gill arches in fish embryos. Adult chickens and adult mammals do not have gills, but this embryonic homology indicates that birds and mammals share a common ancestor with fish. As another example, some species of toothless whales have embryos that initially develop teeth that are later absorbed, which indicates that these whales have an ancestor with teeth in the adult form. Finally, most tetrapods have five-digit limbs, but birds have three-digit limbs in their wings. However, embryonic birds initially have five-digit limbs in their wings, which develop into a three-digit wing. Tetrapods such as reptiles, mammals, and birds all share a common ancestor with five-digit limbs.

Endosymbiosis Theory

The endosymbiosis theory is foundational to evolution. Endosymbiosis provides the path for prokaryotes to give rise to eukaryotes. Specifically, **endosymbiosis** explains the development of the organelles of mitochondria in animals and chloroplasts in plants. This theory states that some eukaryotic organelles such as mitochondria and chloroplasts originated as free living cells. According to this theory, primitive, heterotrophic eukaryotes engulfed smaller, autotrophic bacteria prokaryotes, but the bacteria were not digested. Instead, the eukaryotes and the bacteria formed a symbiotic relationship. Eventually, the bacteria transformed into mitochondrion or chloroplasts.

Supporting Evidence

Several facts support the endosymbiosis theory. Mitochondria and chloroplasts contain their own DNA and can both only arise from other preexisting mitochondria and chloroplasts. The genomes of mitochondria and chloroplasts consist of single, circular DNA molecules with no histones. This is similar to bacteria genomes, not eukaryote genomes. Also, the RNA, ribosomes, and protein synthesis of mitochondria and chloroplasts are remarkably similar to those of bacteria, and both use oxygen to produce ATP. These organelles have a double phospholipid layer that is typical of engulfed bacteria. This theory also involves a secondary endosymbiosis in which the original eukaryotic cells that have engulfed the bacteria are then engulfed themselves by another free-living eukaryote.

Convergent Evolution

Convergent evolution is the evolutionary process in which two or more unrelated species become increasingly similar in appearance. In convergent evolution, similar adaptations in these unrelated species occur due to these species inhabiting the same kind of environment. For example, the mammals shown below, although found in different parts of the world, developed similar appearances due to their similar environments.

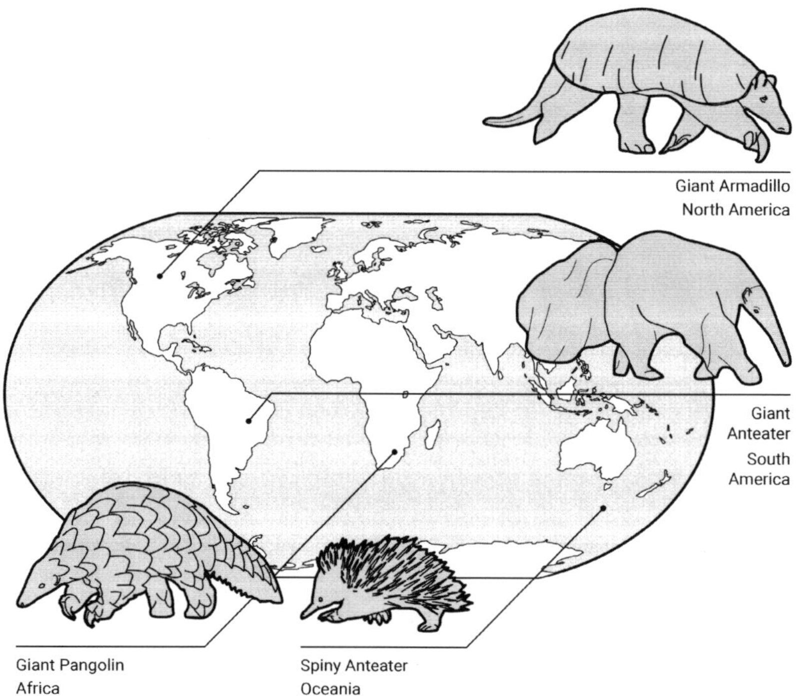

Divergent Evolution

Divergent evolution is the evolutionary process in which organisms of one species become increasingly dissimilar in appearance. As several small adaptations occur due to natural selection, the organisms will finally reach a point at which two new species are formed, also known as **speciation**. Then, these two species will further diverge from each other as they continue to evolve. Adaptive radiation is an example of divergent evolution. Another example is the divergent evolution of the wooly mammoth and the modern elephant from a common ancestor.

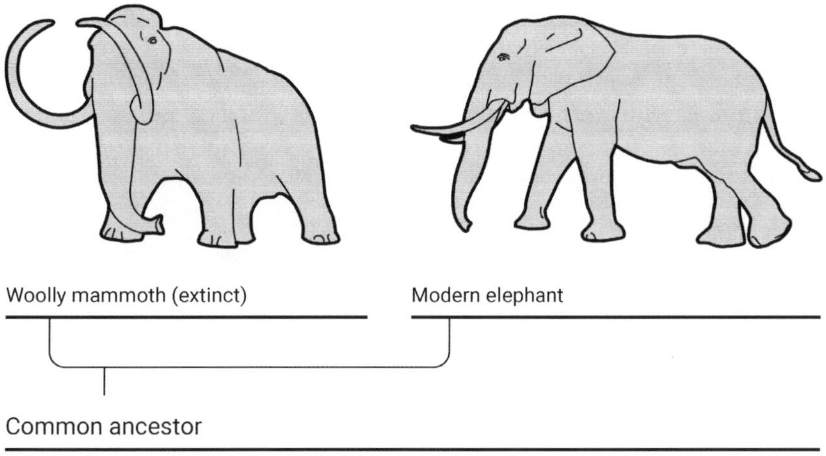

Fossil Record

The **fossil record** provides many types of support for evolution including comparisons from rock layers, transition fossils, and homologies with modern organisms. First, fossils from rock layers from all over the world have been compared, enabling scientists to develop a sequence of life from simple to complex. Based on the fossil record, the **geologic timeline** chronicles the history of all living things. For example, the fossil record clearly indicates that invertebrates developed before vertebrates and that fish developed before amphibians. Second, numerous transitional fossils have been found. **Transitional fossils** show an intermediate state between an ancestral form of an organism and the form of its descendants. These fossils show the path of evolutionary change. For example, many transition fossils documenting the evolutionary change from fish to amphibians have been discovered. In 2004, scientists discovered *Tiktaalik roseae*, or the "fishapod," which is a 375-million-year-old fossil that exhibits both fish and amphibian characteristics. Another example would be *Pakicetus,* an extinct land mammal, that scientists determined is an early ancestor of modern whales and dolphins based on the specialized structures of the inner ear. Most fossils exhibit homologies with modern organisms. For example, extinct horses are similar to modern horses, indicating a common ancestor.

Cephalization and Multicellularity

Cephalization is the evolutionary trend that can be summarized as "the evolution of the head." In most animals, nerve tissue has been concentrated into a brain at one end of an organism over many generations. Eventually, a head enclosing a brain and housing sensory organs was produced at one end of the organism. Many invertebrates, such as arthropods and annelids and all vertebrates, have undergone cephalization. However, some invertebrates, such as echinoderms and sponges, have not undergone cephalization, and these organisms literally do not have a head.

Another evolutionary trend is **multicellularity**. Life has evolved from simple, single-celled organisms to complex, multicellular organisms. Over millions of years, single-celled organisms gave rise to biofilms, which gave rise to multicellular organisms, which gave rise to all of the major phyla of multicellular organisms present today.

Scientific Explanations for the Origin of Life on Earth

Explanations for the Origin of Life on Earth

Panspermia

The word *panspermia* is a Greek work that means "seeds everywhere." **Panspermia** is one possible explanation for the origin of life on Earth that states that "seeds" of life exist throughout the universe and can be transferred from one location to another. Three types of panspermia based on the seed-dispersal method have been proposed. **Lithopanspermia** is described as rocks or dust transferring microorganisms between solar systems. **Ballistic panspermia** is described as rocks or dust transferring microorganisms between planets within the same solar system. **Directed panspermia** is described as intelligent extraterrestrials purposely spreading the seeds to other planets and solar systems. The panspermia hypothesis only proposes the origin of life on Earth. It does not offer an explanation for the origin of life in the universe or explain the origin of the seeds themselves.

Abiotic Synthesis of Organic Compounds

Scientists have performed sophisticated experiments to determine how the first organic compounds appeared on Earth. First, scientists performed controlled experiments that closely resembled the conditions similar to an early Earth. In the classic **Miller–Urey experiment** (1953), the Earth's early atmosphere was simulated with water, methane, ammonia, and hydrogen that were stimulated by an electric discharge. The Miller–Urey experiment produced complex organic compounds including several amino acids, sugars, and hydrocarbons. Later experiments by other scientists produced nucleic acids. Recently, Jeffrey Bada, a former student of Miller, was able to produce amino acids in a simulation using the Earth's current atmospheric conditions with the addition of iron and carbonate to the simulation. This is significant because in previous studies using Earth's current atmosphere, the amino acids were destroyed by the nitrites produced by the nitrogen.

Atmospheric Composition

The early atmosphere of Earth had little or possibly no oxygen. Early rocks had high levels of iron at their surfaces. Without oxygen, the iron just entered into the early oceans as ions. In the same time frame, early photosynthetic algae were beginning to grow abundantly in the early ocean. During photosynthesis, the algae would produce oxygen gas, which oxidized the iron at the rocks' surfaces, forming an iron oxide. This process basically kept the algae in an oxygen-free environment. As the algae population grew much larger, it eventually produced such a large amount of oxygen that it could not be removed by the iron in the rocks. Because the algae at this time were intolerant to oxygen, the algae became extinct. Over time, a new iron-rich layer of sediments formed, and algae populations reformed, and the cycle began again. This cycle repeated itself for millions of years. Iron-rich layers of sediment alternated with iron-poor layers. Gradually, algae and other life forms evolved that were tolerant to oxygen, stabilizing the oxygen concentration in the atmosphere at levels similar to those of today.

Development of Self-Replication

Several hypotheses for the origin of life involve the self-replication of molecules. In order for life to have originated on Earth, proteins and RNA must have been replicated. Hypotheses that combine the replication of proteins and RNA seem promising. One such hypothesis is called **RNA world**. RNA world explains how the pathway of DNA to RNA to protein may have originated by proposing the reverse process. RNA world proposes that self-replicating RNA was the precursor to DNA. Scientists have shown that RNA can actually function both as a gene and as an enzyme and could therefore have carried genetic information in earlier life stages. Also, RNA can be transcribed into DNA using reverse transcription. In RNA world, RNA molecules self-replicated and evolved through recombination and mutations. RNA molecules developed the ability to act as enzymes. Eventually, RNA began to synthesize proteins. Finally, DNA molecules were copied from the RNA in a process of reverse transcription.

Chapter Quiz

Ready to see how well you retained what you just read? Scan the QR code to go directly to the chapter quiz interface for this study guide. If you're using a computer, simply visit the online resources page at **mometrix.com/resources719/ssreglivingenv** and click the Chapter Quizzes link.

Ecology

Hierarchical Structure of the Biosphere

Biosphere

Components

The **biosphere** is the region of the earth inhabited by living things. The components of the biosphere from smallest to largest are organisms, populations, communities, ecosystems, and biomes. Organisms of the same species make up a **population**. All of the populations in an area make up the **community**. The community combined with the physical environment for a region forms an **ecosystem**. Several ecosystems are grouped together to form large geographic regions called **biomes**.

Population

A **population** is a group of all the individuals of one species in a specific area or region at a certain time. A **species** is a group of organisms that can breed and produce fertile offspring. There may be many populations of a specific species in a large geographic region. **Ecologists** study the size, density, and growth rate of populations to determine their stability. Population size continuously changes with births, deaths, and migrations. The population density is the number of individuals per unit of area. Growth rates for a population may be exponential or logistic. Ecologists also study how the individuals are dispersed within a population. Some species form clusters, while others are evenly or randomly spaced. However, every population has limiting factors. Changes in the environment or geography can reduce or limit population size. The individuals of a population interact with each other and with other organisms in the community in various ways, including competition and predation, which have direct impacts population size.

Community Interactions

A **community** is all of the populations of different species that live in an area and interact with each other. Community interaction can be intraspecific or interspecific. **Intraspecific interactions** occur between members of the same species. **Interspecific interactions** occur between members of different species. Different types of interactions include competition, predation, and symbiosis. Communities with high diversity are more complex and more stable than communities with low diversity. The level of diversity can be seen in a food web of the community, which shows all the feeding relationships within the community.

Ecosystems

An **ecosystem** is the basic unit of ecology. An ecosystem is the sum of all the biotic and abiotic factors in an area. **Biotic factors** are all living things such as plants, animals, fungi, and microorganisms. **Abiotic factors** include the light, water, air, temperature, and soil in an area. Ecosystems obtain the energy they need from sunlight. Ecosystems also contain biogeochemical cycles such as the hydrologic cycle and the nitrogen cycle. Ecosystems are generally classified as either terrestrial or aquatic. All of the living things within an ecosystem are called its community. The number and variety of living things within a community describes the ecosystem's **biodiversity**. However, each ecosystem can only support a limited number of organisms known as the **carrying capacity**.

Relationships between Species

Symbiosis

Many species share a special nutritional relationship with another species, called **symbiosis**. The term symbiosis means "living together." In symbiosis, two organisms share a close physical relationship that can be helpful, harmful, or neutral for each organism. Three forms of symbiotic relationships are parasitism, commensalism, and mutualism. **Parasitism** is a relationship between two organisms in which one organism is the parasite, and the other organism is the host. The parasite benefits from the relationship because the parasite obtains its nutrition from the host. The host is harmed from the relationship because the parasite is using the host's energy and giving nothing in return. For example, a tick and a dog share a parasitic relationship in which the tick is the parasite, and the dog is the host. **Commensalism** is a relationship between two organisms in which one benefits, and the other is not affected. For example, a small fish called a remora can attach to the belly of a shark and ride along. The remora is safe under the shark, and the shark is not affected. **Mutualism** is a relationship between two organisms in which both organisms benefit. For example, a rhinoceros usually can be seen with a few tick birds perched on its back. The tick birds are helped by the easy food source of ticks, and the rhino benefits from the tick removal.

Predation

Predation is a special nutritional relationship in which one organism is the predator, and the other organism is the prey. The predator benefits from the relationship, but the prey is harmed. The predator hunts and kills the prey for food. The predator is specially adapted to hunt its prey, and the prey is specially adapted to escape its predator. While predators harm (kill) their individual prey, predation usually helps the prey species. Predation keeps the population of the prey species under control and prevents them from overshooting the carrying capacity, which often leads to starvation. Also, predation usually helps to remove weak or slow members of the prey species leaving the healthier, stronger, and better adapted individuals to reproduce. Examples of predator-prey relationships include lions and zebras, snakes and rats, and hawks and rabbits.

Competition and Territoriality

Competition is a relationship between two organisms in which the organisms compete for the same vital resource that is in short supply. Typically, both organisms are harmed, but one is usually harmed more than the other, which provides an avenue for natural selection. Organisms compete for resources such as food, water, mates, and space. **Interspecific competition** is between members of different species, while **intraspecific competition** is between members of the same species. **Territoriality** can be considered to be a type of interspecific competition for space. Many animals including mammals, birds, reptiles, fish, spiders, and insects have exhibited territorial behavior. Once territories are established, there are fewer conflicts between organisms. For example, a male redwing blackbird can establish a large territory. By singing and flashing his red patches, he is able to warn other males to avoid his territory, and they can avoid fighting.

Altruistic Behaviors Between Animals

Altruism is a self-sacrificing behavior in which an individual animal may serve or protect another animal. For example, in a honey bee colony there is one queen with many workers (females). There are also drones (males), but only during the mating seasons. Adult workers do all the work of the hive and will die defending it. Another example of altruism is seen in a naked mole rat colony. Each colony has one queen that mates with a few males, and the rest of the colony is nonbreeding and lives to service the queen, her mates, and her offspring.

> **Review Video: Mutualism, Commensalism, and Parasitism**
> Visit mometrix.com/academy and enter code: 757249

Energy Flow in the Environment

Using Trophic Levels with an Energy Pyramid

Energy flow through an ecosystem can be tracked through an energy pyramid. An **energy pyramid** shows how energy is transferred from one trophic level to another. **Producers** always form the base of an energy pyramid, and the consumers form successive levels above the producers. Producers only store about 1% of the solar energy they receive. Then, each successive level only uses about 10% of the energy of the previous level. That means that **primary consumers** use about 10% of the energy used by primary producers, such as grasses and trees. Next, **secondary consumers** use 10% of primary consumers' 10%, or 1% overall. This continues up for as many trophic levels as exist in a particular ecosystem.

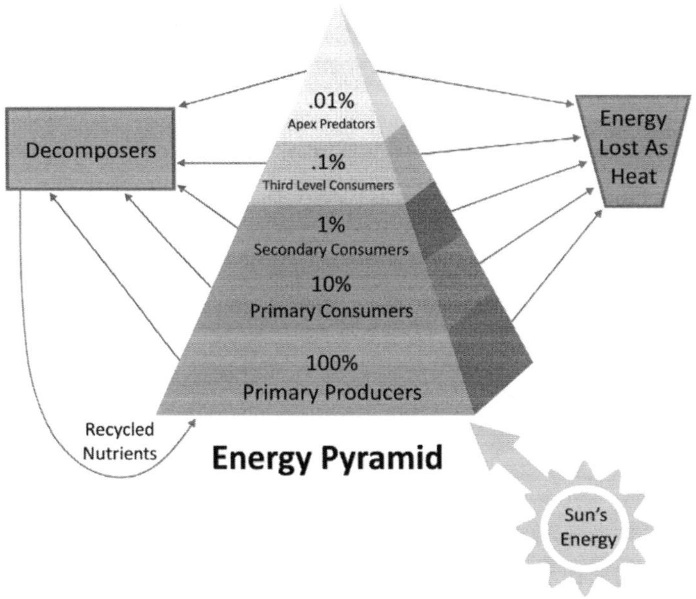

Food Web

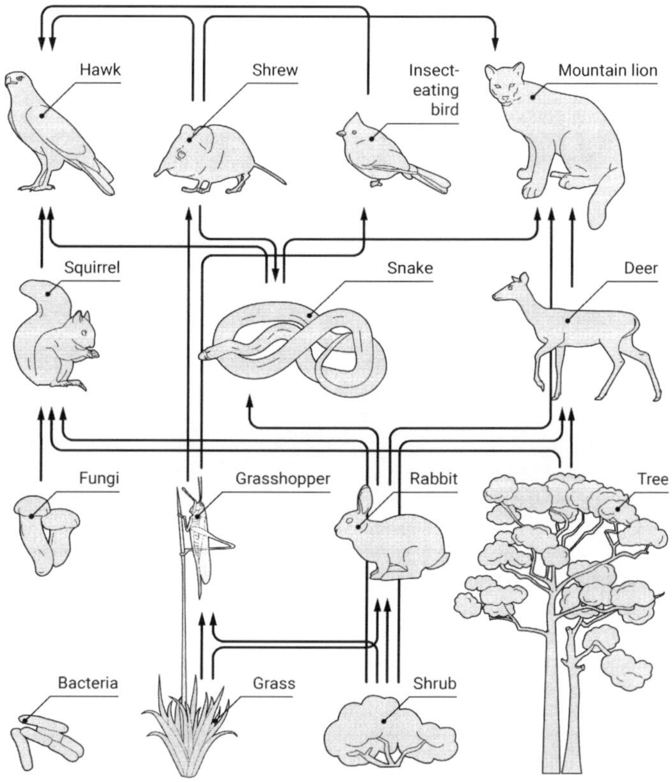

Energy flow through an ecosystem can be illustrated by a **food web**. Energy moves through the food web in the direction of the arrows. In the food web, producers such as grass, trees, and shrubs use energy from the sun to produce food through photosynthesis. Herbivores or primary consumers such as squirrels, grasshoppers, and rabbits obtain energy by eating the producers. Secondary consumers, which are carnivores such as snakes and shrews, obtain energy by eating the primary consumers. Tertiary consumers, which are carnivores such as hawks and mountain lions, obtain energy by eating the secondary consumers. Note that the hawk and the mountain lion can also be considered quaternary consumers in this food web if a different food chain within the web is followed.

Review Video: Food Webs
Visit mometrix.com/academy and enter code: 853254

Biogeochemical Cycles

Water Cycle

The water cycle, also referred to as the **hydrologic cycle**, is a biogeochemical cycle that describes the continuous movement of the Earth's water. Water in the form of **precipitation** such as rain or snow moves from the atmosphere to the ground. The water is collected in oceans, lakes, rivers, and other bodies of water. Heat from the sun then causes water to **evaporate** from those oceans, lakes, rivers, and other bodies of water. As plants transpire, this water also undergoes evaporation. This water vapor collects in the sky and forms clouds. As the water vapor in the clouds cools, the water vapor **condenses** or sublimes depending on the conditions. Then, water moves back to the ground in the form of precipitation.

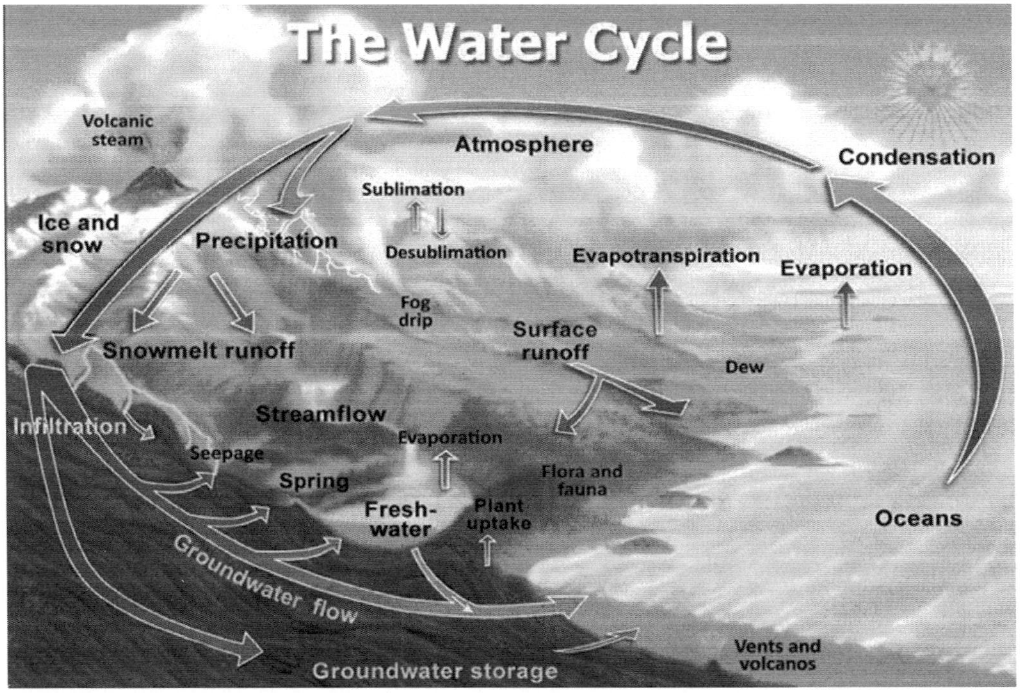

Carbon Cycle

The **carbon cycle** is a biogeochemical cycle that describes the continuous movement of the Earth's carbon. Carbon is in the atmosphere, the soil, living organisms, fossil fuels, oceans, and freshwater systems. These areas are referred to as **carbon reservoirs**. Carbon flows between these reservoirs in an exchange called the carbon cycle. In the atmosphere, carbon is in the form of carbon dioxide. Carbon moves from the atmosphere to plants through the process of photosynthesis. Carbon moves from plants to animals through food chains, and then moves from living organisms to the soil when these organisms die. Carbon moves from living organisms to the atmosphere through cellular respiration. Carbon moves from fossil fuels to the atmosphere when fossil fuels are burned. Carbon moves from the atmosphere to the oceans and freshwater systems through absorption.

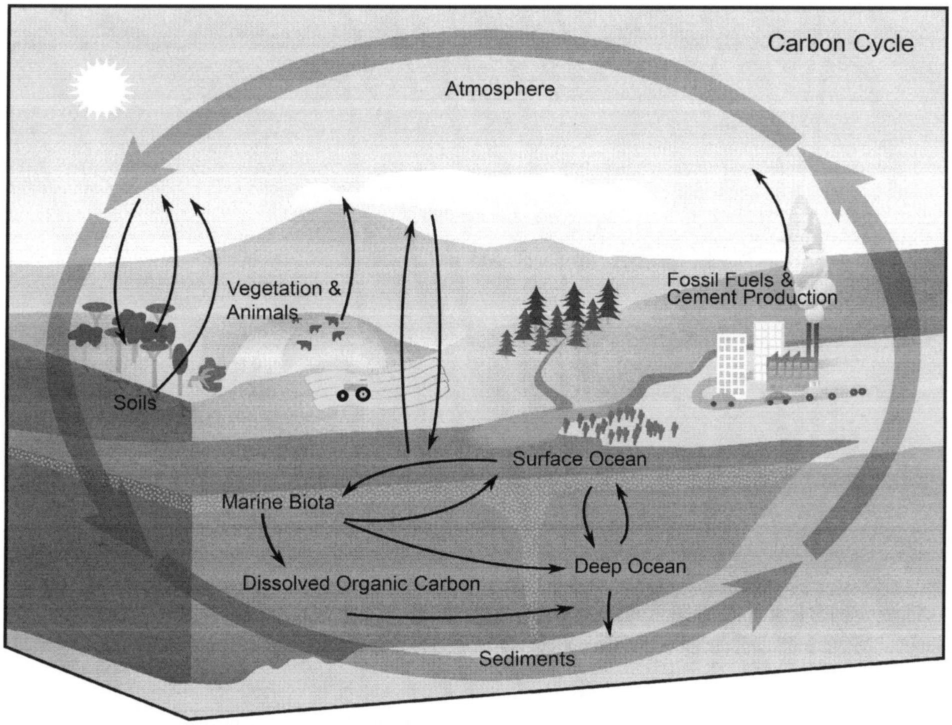

Nitrogen Cycle

The **nitrogen cycle** is a biogeochemical cycle that describes the continuous movement of the Earth's nitrogen. Approximately 78% of the Earth's atmosphere consists of nitrogen in its elemental form N_2. Nitrogen is essential to the formation of proteins, but most organisms cannot use nitrogen in this form and require the nitrogen to be converted into some form of **nitrates**. Lightning can cause nitrates to form in the atmosphere, which can be carried to the soil by rain to be used by plants. Legumes have nitrogen-fixing bacteria in their roots, which can convert the N_2 to ammonia (NH_3). Nitrifying bacteria in the soil can also convert ammonia into nitrates. Plants absorb nitrates from the soil, and animals can consume the plants and other animals for protein. Denitrifying bacteria can convert unused nitrates back to nitrogen to be returned to the atmosphere.

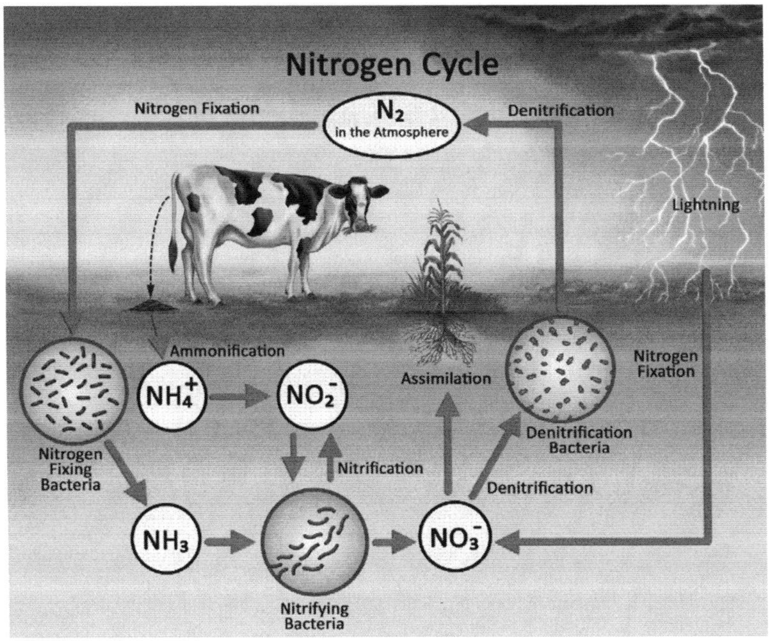

Phosphorus Cycle

The **phosphorus cycle** is a biogeochemical cycle that describes the continuous movement of the Earth's phosphorus. Phosphorus is found in rocks. When these rocks weather and erode, the phosphorus moves into the soil. The phosphorus found in the soil and rocks is in the form of phosphates or compounds with the PO_4^{3-} ion. When it rains, phosphates can be dissolved into the water. Plants are able to use phosphates from the soil. Plants need phosphorus for growth and development. Phosphorus is also a component of DNA, RNA, ATP, cell membranes, and bones. Plants and algae can absorb phosphate ions from the water and convert them into many organic compounds. Animals can get phosphorus by eating food or drinking water. When organisms die, the phosphorus is returned to the soil. This is the slowest of all biogeochemical cycles.

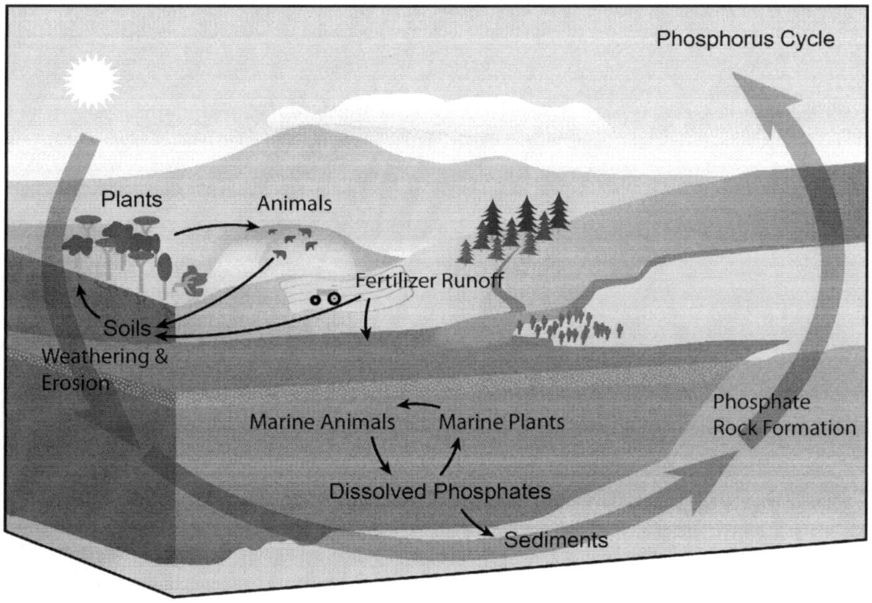

Chapter Quiz

Ready to see how well you retained what you just read? Scan the QR code to go directly to the chapter quiz interface for this study guide. If you're using a computer, simply visit the online resources page at **mometrix.com/resources719/ssreglivingenv** and click the Chapter Quizzes link.

Practice Test #1

Want to take this practice test in an online interactive format?
Check out the online resources page, which includes interactive practice questions and much more: **mometrix.com/resources719/ssreglivingenv**

1. Scientists have discovered a single-celled organism, and need to classify it as either a prokaryote or a eukaryote. Which of the following structures, if present, would indicate that the organism is a eukaryote?

a. mitochondria
b. DNA
c. plasma membrane
d. cytoplasm

2. Cell membranes are selectively permeable. Some solutes move freely across cell membranes, while other solutes require assistance from special gates. Passive transport and active transport are methods of moving solutes across cell membranes. Which of the following accurately describes the difference between passive transport and active transport?

a. Passive transport can move molecules both in and out of a cell, but active transport cannot.
b. Passive transport works against a concentration gradient, but active transport does not.
c. Passive transport does not require energy, but active transport does.
d. Passive transport requires carrier proteins, but active transport does not.

3. The U.S. Centers for Disease Control released this 3-D graphical representation of the H1N1 influenza virus. Approximately five million Americans were infected with this virus during a four-month period in 2009.

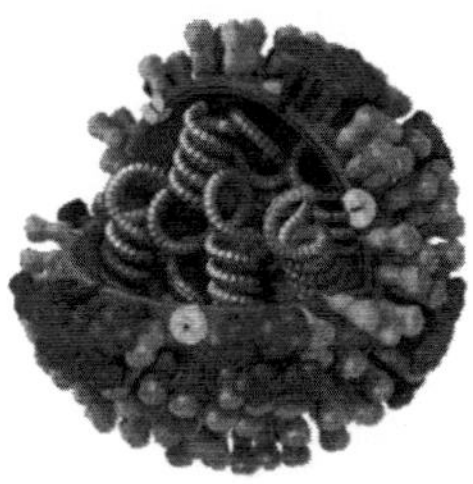

Which of the following is NOT true of the H1N1 virus?

a. It cannot reproduce on its own.
b. It lacks ribosomes.
c. It lacks both DNA and RNA.
d. It does not grow or undergo division.

4. During human fertilization, a single-celled zygote is formed. This cell divides, and the daughter cells continue to divide until an embryo is formed.

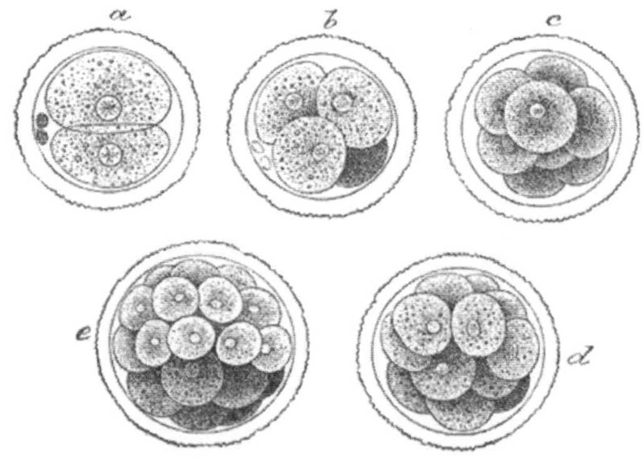

Which of the following BEST describes this process of cell division?

a. It produces daughter cells with half the number of chromosomes as the parent cell.
b. It takes place during the S phase of interphase.
c. It takes place during the G1 phase of interphase.
d. It produces daughter cells with the same number of chromosomes as the parent cell.

5. Most of the cells in the human body continually undergo mitosis so that dead or damaged cells can be replaced. The diagram below shows the phases of mitosis.

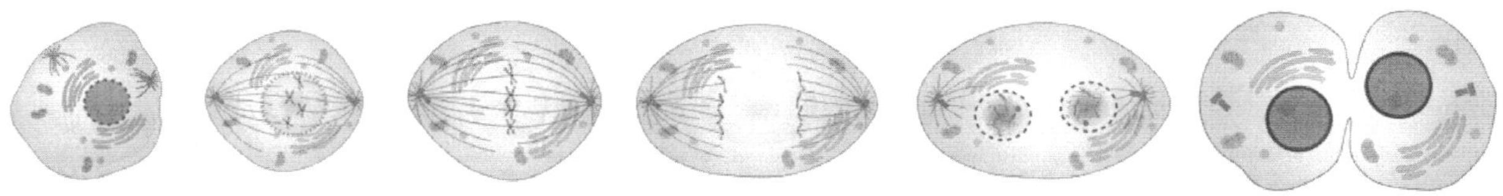

Which of the following lists the four basic phases of mitosis in the order in which they occur?

a. prophase, metaphase, anaphase, telophase
b. interphase, prophase, anaphase, telophase
c. interphase, metaphase, prophase, telophase
d. metaphase, anaphase, telophase, prophase

6. The nervous system of an adult human consists of more than one billion nerve cells. The diagram below shows a typical neuron.

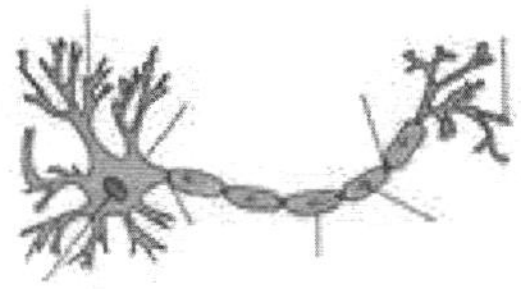

Which of the following BEST describes the functions of the neuron's structures?

a. Dendrites carry impulses toward the cell body, and axons carry impulses away from the cell body.
b. Axons carry impulses toward the cell body, and dendrites carry impulses away from the cell body.
c. Both dendrites and axons carry impulses toward the cell body.
d. Both dendrites and axons carry impulses away from the cell body.

7. Which of the following is NOT a difference between normal cell division and cancer cell division?

a. Normal cells recognize signals that tell them to stop and start the cell cycle, but cancer cells do not.
b. Normal cells can invade other tissues, but cancer cells cannot.
c. In normal cells DNA is replicated correctly, but in cancer cells DNA is mutated.
d. Normal cells communicate with each other, but cancer cells do not.

8. Pepsin is an enzyme produced by the lining of the stomach that aids in the digestion of proteins. Which of the following BEST describes the role of pepsin in protein digestion?

a. Pepsin separates the nucleotides in base pairs.
b. Pepsin severs the peptide bonds between amino acids.
c. Pepsin separates the glycerol from fatty acids.
d. Pepsin separates the glucose from fructose.

9. Scientists often form hypotheses based on particular observations. Which of the following is NOT true of a good hypothesis?

a. A good hypothesis is complex.
b. A good hypothesis is testable.
c. A good hypothesis is logical.
d. A good hypothesis predicts future events.

10. During a lab activity, a biology student was instructed to examine various prepared slides under a microscope. The student noted his observations in the chart below.

Observation	Slide 1	Slide 2	Slide 3
Nuclear Membrane	Yes	No	Yes
Cell Membrane	Yes	Yes	Yes
Cell Wall	No	Yes	Yes
Chloroplast	No	No	Yes
Ribosome	Yes	Yes	Yes

Which of the following is a valid conclusion based on the student's observations?

a. Slides 1 and 2 are slides of eukaryotes, and slide 3 is a slide of a prokaryote.
b. All three slides are slides of eukaryotes.
c. Slides 1 and 3 are slides of eukaryotes, and slide 2 is a slide of a prokaryote.
d. Slides 1 and 3 are slides of prokaryotes, and slide 2 is a slide of a eukaryote.

11. A biology student completes a science fair project. The purpose of the student's project is to study the effect of soil pH on a specific type of tomato plant. She divides forty plants into four groups of ten, using one group as the control. She records her results in the table below.

Soil pH	Number of surviving plants (out of the original 10)
7	10
5	8
3	0
1	0

Which of the following is the BEST conclusion about the type of tomato plant the student used in this experiment based on the results shown in the table?

a. This type of tomato plant does best in basic soil.
b. This type of tomato plant does best in acidic soil.
c. This type of tomato plant does best in neutral soil.
d. This type of tomato plant is not affected by soil pH.

12. Deoxyribonucleic acid, DNA, is primarily found in the nuclei of human cells, and stores an individual's genetic information. Which of the following BEST describes the structure of DNA?

a. DNA is a single helix consisting of sugars, phosphates, and the bases adenine, thymine, guanine, and cytosine.
b. DNA is a single helix consisting of sugars, phosphates, and the bases adenine, uracil, guanine, and cytosine.
c. DNA is a double helix consisting of sugars, phosphates, and the bases adenine, thymine, guanine, and cytosine.
d. DNA is a double helix consisting of sugars, phosphates, and the bases adenine, uracil, guanine, and cytosine.

13. Bacteria are classified as prokaryotes because they do not contain membrane-bound nuclei. Which of the following is true of bacteria and the genetic information they contain?

a. Bacteria do not typically have DNA, but do have RNA.
b. Bacteria have DNA that is stored in plasmids located in the cytoplasm.
c. Bacteria have RNA that is stored in plasmids located in the cytoplasm.
d. Bacteria have DNA, which is typically stored in a single, circular chromosome. Some bacteria also have additional DNA in plasmids.

14. In order to survive, cells need to be able to successfully process, duplicate, and use the genetic information contained in their DNA molecules. Which of the following BEST describes the process of transcription?

a. During transcription, the cell copies genetic information from an RNA molecule onto a different RNA molecule.
b. During transcription, the cell copies genetic information from one DNA molecule onto a different DNA molecule.
c. During transcription, the cell copies genetic information from a DNA molecule onto an RNA molecule.
d. During transcription, the cell copies genetic information from an RNA molecule onto a DNA molecule.

15. Gene expression is a highly regulated process. Which of the following BEST describes the starting point of this process?

a. Gene expression begins with the transcription of a DNA molecule to an RNA molecule.
b. Gene expression begins with the translation of amino acids into a protein molecule.
c. Gene expression begins with the translocation of nonhomologous chromosomes.
d. Gene expression begins with point mutations of specific nucleotides.

16. Random and permanent changes in DNA are called mutations. Which of the following is the term used to describe a mutation in which a segment of a chromosome breaks off and reattaches in the same position, but the order of the genes is reversed?

a. substitution
b. translocation
c. inversion
d. deletion

17. In the 1900s, Gregor Mendel, an Austrian monk, experimented with pea plants in his garden. The Punnett square below shows the genetic combinations that could have resulted when he crossed a pure tall pea plant (TT) with a hybrid tall pea plant (Tt).

	T	**T**
T	TT	TT
t	Tt	??

Which of the following correctly completes the square?

a. TT
b. tt
c. Tt
d. none of the above

18. Hedgehogs have 88 chromosomes in their somatic cells. If one of these cells undergoes meiotic cell division, how many chromosomes will each daughter cell contain?

a. 88
b. 44
c. 176
d. 22

19. Black hair is dominant over white hair in rabbits. If a heterozygous, black-haired male is crossed with a white-haired female, what is the probability that their offspring will have white hair?

a. 100%
b. 75%
c. 50%
d. 0%

20. Certain flowers exhibit non-Mendelian inheritance patterns. Japanese four o'clock plants exhibit incomplete dominance. If a Japanese four o'clock plant with red flowers is crossed with a Japanese four o'clock plant with white flowers, what will MOST LIKELY be the outcome?

a. All of the offspring will have pink flowers.
b. All of the offspring will have red flowers.
c. All of the offspring will have white flowers.
d. Half of the offspring will have red flowers, and half will have white flowers.

21. Which of the following is MOST associated with the stage of mitosis known as metaphase?

a. The cell's chromosomes are lined up along the equatorial plane.
b. The nucleolus is dismantled.
c. The chromatids are moved to opposite ends of the cell.
d. The cell's DNA is replicated.

22. Which of the following is true of skeletal muscle tissue?

a. Skeletal muscle tissue consists of elongated, spindle-shaped cells, each of which contains a single nucleus.
b. Skeletal muscle tissue consists of cross-striated, quadrangular cells, each of which contains a single nucleus.
c. Skeletal muscle tissue consists of striated, cylindrical fibers, each of which contains nuclei located towards the outer edges of the fiber.
d. Skeletal muscle tissue consists of tightly packed, cuboidal cells, each of which contains a single nucleus.

23. Comparison of the anatomy of different species of mammals reveals that many mammals have similar skeletal structures. Which of the following is the MOST LIKELY explanation for these similarities?

a. The similarities are most likely due to similar reproductive processes.
b. The similarities are most likely due to a common ancestor.
c. The similarities are most likely due to a common environment.
d. The similarities are most likely due to a common food source.

24. The Northern Flicker is a medium-sized member of the woodpecker family. Red-shafted flickers live on the West Coast, and yellow-shafted flickers live on the East Coast. Which of the following is the MOST LIKELY explanation for these color differences?

a. The color differences are most likely due to natural selection.
b. The color differences are most likely due to different ancestors.
c. The color differences are most likely due to different environments.
d. The color differences are most likely due to different food sources.

25. Two companion models, gradualism and punctuated equilibrium, dominate evolutionary theory. Which of the following statements is most consistent with the theory of punctuated equilibrium?

a. Fossils show changes over large periods of time.
b. Fossils showing intermediate characteristics may not necessarily be found.
c. Speciation occurs gradually.
d. Evolution is a slow, steady process.

26. Carolus Linneaus was a Swedish naturalist who devised the binomial naming system used in taxonomy today. According to the seven category system devised by Linnaeus, which of the following is the broadest category?

a. order
b. genus
c. family
d. class

27. Today, many biologists classify organisms as members of one of six kingdoms: Animalia, Plantae, Fungi, Protista, Archaea, and Bacteria. Which of the following is true of organisms that are part of Kingdom Plantae (plants)?

a. They are multicellular and autotrophic.
b. They are multicellular and heterotrophic.
c. They are unicellular and autotrophic.
d. They are unicellular and heterotrophic.

28. According to modern taxonomic classification, which of the following organisms are MOST CLOSELY related?

a. roses and toadstools
b. Gila monsters and clams
c. bacteria and paramecia
d. sponges and bacteria

29. If an individual was describing various organisms using a six kingdom classification system, which of the following statements would BEST describe fungi?

a. All fungi are unicellular heterotrophs.
b. All fungi are macroscopic, and use spores to reproduce.
c. All fungi are heterotrophs, and use spores to reproduce.
d. All fungi are unicellular decomposers.

30. All organisms can be classified as either prokaryotic or eukaryotic. Which of the following kingdoms contain ONLY eukaryotes?

a. Bacteria and Protista
b. Bacteria and Archaea
c. Protista and Fungi
d. Fungi and Archaea

31. Many organisms have some of the same characteristics. Which of the following terms is used to describe shared characteristics that are due to a common ancestor?

a. homogenous
b. heterogeneous
c. heterologous
d. homologous

32. The diagram below is a modern form of the tree of life based on genetic analyses.

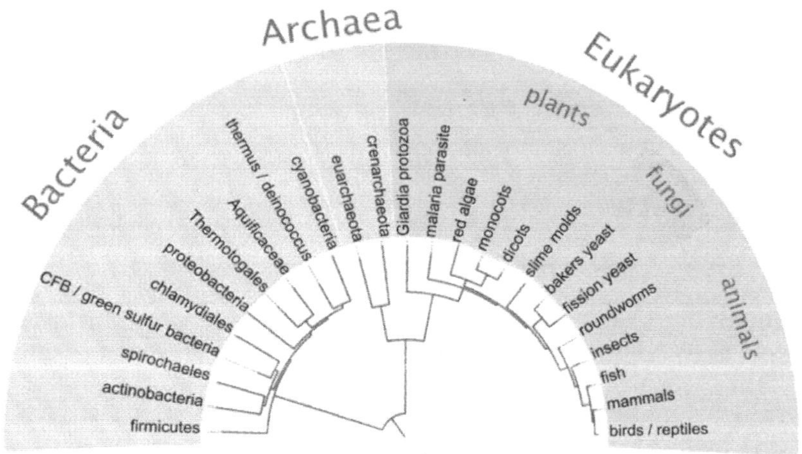

According to this diagram, which of the following groups of organisms have the MOST SIMILAR evolutionary history?

a. red algae and baker's yeast
b. insects and slime molds
c. monocots and dicots
d. firmicutes and euryarchaeota

33. Photosynthesis is a complex process that produces glucose for plants. Which of the following is the source of the carbon found in these glucose molecules?

a. carbon monoxide in the air
b. carbon dioxide in the air
c. carbon atoms from organic material in the soil
d. carbon atoms from minerals in ground water

34. Enzymes play an important role in the processes that help organisms stay healthy and survive. Which of the following best describes enzymes?

a. Enzymes are protein molecules that act as biological catalysts.
b. Enzymes are fat-soluble organic compounds with specific physiological functions.
c. Enzymes are strong acids that break down large biomolecules.
d. Enzymes are lipids that store energy.

35. All animal cells need nutrients to survive. Which of the following BEST explains what happens to nutrients once they cross the cell membrane?

a. Nutrients are transported by proteins to the nucleus for storage.
b. Nutrients are transported by proteins to a Golgi complex for packaging and shipping.
c. Nutrients are transported by proteins to mitochondria to be processed into glucose and ATP.
d. Nutrients are transported to the ribosomes to build proteins.

36. Biomass pyramids, energy pyramids, and number pyramids are visual representations of information about ecosystems. Which of the following statements is true of biomass pyramids?

a. Biomass pyramids show the total energy flow in an ecosystem.
b. Biomass pyramids are never inverted.
c. Biomass pyramids are inverted for aquatic ecosystems.
d. Biomass pyramids indicate the number of each type of organism in an ecosystem.

37. Camels have many adaptations that enable them to survive in their harsh desert environment.

Which of the following adaptations would MOST LIKELY protect camels from blowing sand?

a. two rows of long eyelashes
b. fat stored in the hump
c. thick, leathery patches on the knees
d. thick fur and under wool

38. Plants and animals have several levels of organization. Which of the following is a correct statement about these levels of organization?

a. Tissues make up cells, which make up organs.
b. Cells make up organs, which make up tissues.
c. Organs make up tissues, which make up cells.
d. Cells make up tissues, which make up organs.

39. During a laboratory investigation, students examined the effect of carbon dioxide concentration on the rate of photosynthesis in an aquatic plant. Students took 20 stems from an aquatic plant and submerged them in separate test tubes of pond water. Sodium bicarbonate was added to 10 of the test tubes to increase the level of carbon dioxide in the tubes. All test tubes were placed 10 cm away from the light source. The rate of photosynthesis was determined by counting the number of bubbles produced in one minute. The number of bubbles counted by both groups was averaged, and the results were recorded in the table below.

Average number of bubbles produced in one minute (no sodium bicarbonate added to test tube)	Average number of bubbles produced in one minute (sodium bicarbonate added to test tube)
190	252

Which of the following inferences can be made based on the information provided above?

a. The rate of photosynthesis increases exponentially as carbon dioxide levels increase.
b. The rate of photosynthesis is unaffected by increases in carbon dioxide levels.
c. The rate of photosynthesis increases as the concentration of carbon dioxide increases.
d. The rate of photosynthesis decreases as the concentration of carbon dioxide increases.

40. Which of the following is NOT true of photosynthesis?

a. Every step of photosynthesis requires light.
b. Carbon dioxide enters the plant through stomata in the leaves and stems.
c. Water enters the plant through the root hairs in the soil.
d. Water may be produced during photosynthesis.

41. The transportation system in angiosperms consists of the vascular tissues xylem and phloem. Which of the following is true of xylem and phloem?

a. Xylem transports water and carbon dioxide up from the roots, and phloem transports oxygen down to the rest of the plant.
b. Xylem transports water and minerals up from the roots, and phloem transports glucose down to the rest of the plant.
c. Phloem transports water and carbon dioxide up from the roots, and xylem transports oxygen down to the rest of the plant.
d. Phloem transports water and minerals up from the roots, and xylem transports glucose down to the rest of the plant.

42. During a botany project, a student placed a clear plastic bag over a green potted plant for three days. Which of the following hypotheses might the student be trying to test?

a. Plants produce glucose during photosynthesis.
b. The color of light affects photosynthesis.
c. The amount of water a plant receives affects photosynthesis.
d. Plants lose water via transpiration through their leaves.

43. A group of biology students is investigating tropisms in plants. They are instructed to cut the tips off of nine radish seedlings and place them in petri dishes. Three of the seedlings have tips that are pointing down, three have tips that are pointing horizontally, and three have tips that are pointing up. Which of the following tropisms might the students be trying to investigate?

a. thigmotropism
b. phototropism
c. hydrotropism
d. gravitropism

44. Ecosystems are dynamic, and various factors—both biotic and abiotic—can have serious effects on their stability. Which of the following lists ONLY abiotic factors that can affect ecosystems?

a. temperature, soil pH, and types of producers
b. oxygen availability, amount of light, and amount of available water
c. floods, types of decomposers, and droughts
d. fires, types of autotrophs, and water salinity

45. Microorganisms play a vital role in Earth's ecosystems. Diatoms, as shown in the figure below, make up a large part of the phytoplankton in our oceans, lakes, and ponds.

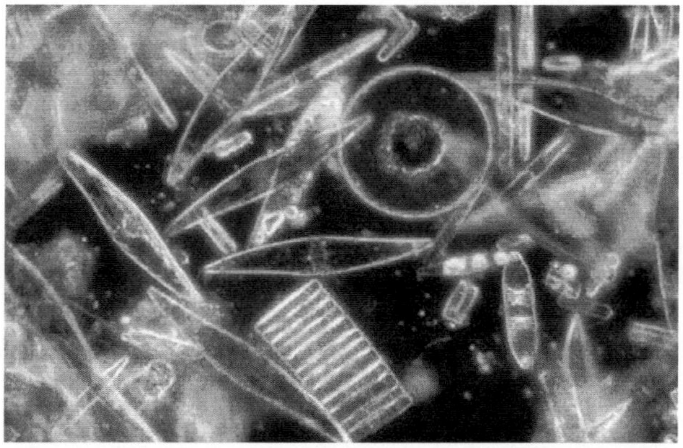

Which of the following describes the typical role of phytoplankton in marine ecosystems?

a. Phytoplankton are primary consumers in nearly all marine food chains.
b. Phytoplankton are secondary consumers in nearly all marine food chains.
c. Phytoplankton are producers in nearly all marine food chains.
d. Phytoplankton are decomposers in nearly all marine food chains.

46. Ecological succession typically begins with a pioneer stage and ends with a climax stage. Which of the following BEST describes organisms in the climax stage?

a. Organisms in the climax stage are typically smaller than organisms in the pioneer stage.
b. Organisms in the climax stage typically have shorter life spans than organisms in the pioneer stage.
c. Organisms in the climax stage typically have simpler life cycles than organisms in the pioneer stage.
d. Organisms in the climax stage typically have lower metabolic rates than organisms in the pioneer stage.

47. Organisms can interact with each other in many different ways in an ecosystem. For example, protozoans that live in the digestive tracts of termites help termites digest the cellulose in the wood that the termites consume. The termites and the protozoa could not survive without each other. Which of the following terms BEST describes this relationship?

a. mutualism
b. neutralism
c. competition
d. amensalism

48. Dolphins can survive because of their many adaptations. Which of the following adaptations helps dolphins conserve the oxygen they need to make long dives?

a. Dolphins work together to herd the fish they consume.
b. A dolphin's tail moves up and down to help propel the dolphin through the water.
c. A dolphin's heart beat slows during long dives, and blood is diverted to vital internal organs.
d. Dolphins have a layer of blubber, which provides insulation.

49. A forest food web is illustrated below.

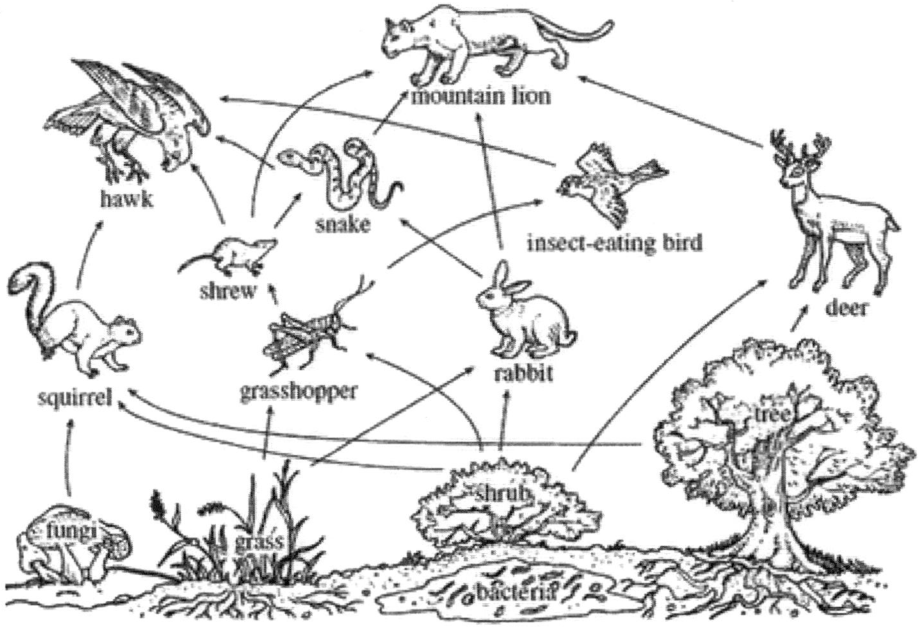

Which of the following describes how energy might flow through this food web?

a. mountain lion → snake → rabbit → shrub
b. squirrel → hawk → shrew → grasshopper
c. shrub → deer → mountain lion → hawk
d. grass → rabbit → snake → mountain lion

50. Ecosystems include herbivores, omnivores, and carnivores. Which of the following identifies the correct trophic level for carnivores?

a. primary consumers
b. secondary consumers
c. producers
d. decomposers

51. In an ecosystem, matter such as oxygen, carbon, and nitrogen is cyclic. Nitrogen is the most abundant of the gases that make up our atmosphere, and undergoes the processes shown in the figure below.

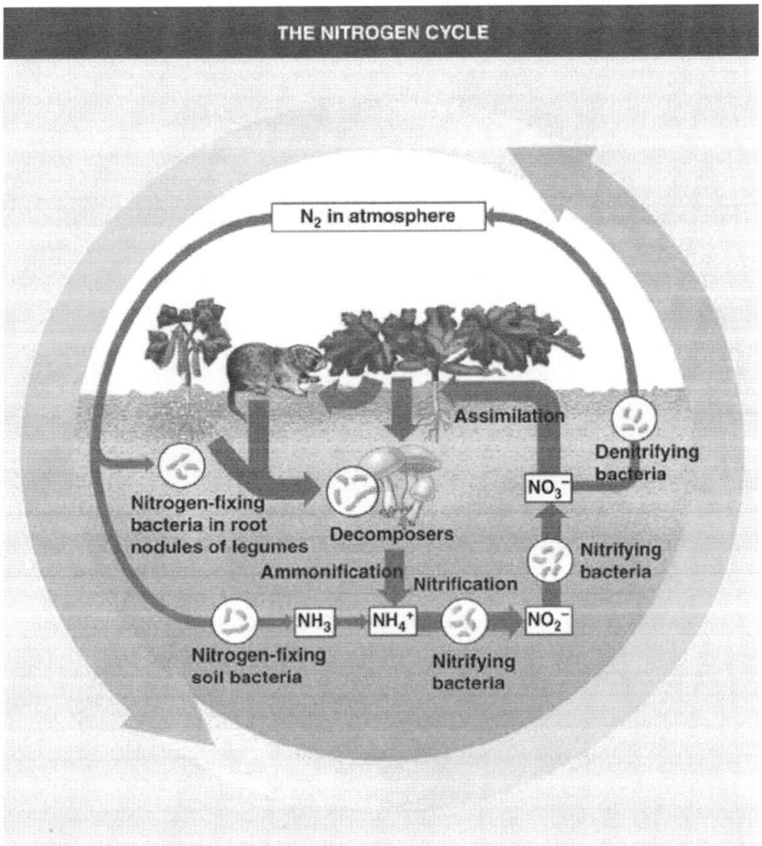

Which of the following is true of the nitrogen cycle?

a. Decomposers convert nitrogen into a form that organisms can use.
b. Nitrogen-fixing bacteria convert nitrogen into a form that organisms can use.
c. Denitrifying bacteria convert nitrogen into a form that organisms can use.
d. Atmospheric nitrogen exists in a form that organisms can use.

52. All organisms on Earth can be arranged into five levels of organization. Which of the following levels includes all of the other levels?

a. ecosystem
b. biosphere
c. population
d. community

53. Krill are small crustaceans that are found in all of the world's oceans. Krill feed on phytoplankton, and are an important food source for many carnivores.

According to the above description, which of the following terms BEST describes krill?

a. tertiary consumers
b. secondary consumers
c. producers
d. primary consumers

54. Ecosystems require energy at every level. Which of the following is NOT true of the energy in an ecosystem?

a. Energy in an ecosystem decreases with each trophic level.
b. Energy in an ecosystem is initially provided by the sun.
c. Energy in an ecosystem may be stored as fats, sugars, and starches.
d. Energy in an ecosystem increases as it moves through each step of a food chain.

Answer Key and Explanations for Test #1

1. A: Both prokaryotic and eukaryotic cells contain DNA and cytoplasm, and both are enclosed by a plasma membrane. This eliminates choices B, C, and D. Prokaryotic cells lack a nucleus and membrane-bound organelles such as mitochondria. Therefore, choice A is correct.

2. C: Both passive transport and active transport can move molecules in and out of cells. Passive transport moves solutes along a concentration gradient, while active transport moves solutes against a concentration gradient. Both passive and active transport require carrier proteins. This eliminates choices A, B, and D. Since active transport moves solutes against a concentration gradient, it requires energy. Passive transport moves solutes along a concentration gradient, and does not require energy. Therefore, choice C is correct.

3. C: Unlike cells, viruses do not reproduce on their own, do not have ribosomes, and do not grow or divide. This eliminates choices A, B, and D. Viruses do contain DNA or RNA (never both). Therefore, H1N1 does NOT lack both DNA and RNA. Therefore, choice C is correct.

4. D: The type of cell division described in this question is mitosis, which occurs after interphase. This eliminates choices B and C. During mitosis, the daughter cells that are produced are identical to the parent cell, and contain the same number of chromosomes. This eliminates choice A. Therefore, choice D is correct.

5. A: Interphase occurs before mitosis. This eliminates choices B and C. The correct order of the phases following interphase is prophase, metaphase, anaphase, and telophase. Therefore, the correct answer is A.

6. A: Electrical impulses flow from the dendrites to the cell body, and then down the axon. Dendrites receive impulses and relay them to the cell body. This eliminates choices B and D. Axons carry impulses away from the cell body. This eliminates choice C. Therefore, the correct answer is A.

7. B: Normal cells recognize signals that tell them to start and stop the cell cycle, they replicate DNA correctly, and they communicate with each other, while cancer cells do not. This eliminates choices A, C, and D. Cancer cells can invade other tissues, but normal cells cannot.

8. B: Choice A refers to nucleotides, which are structural components of nucleic acids, not proteins. Choice C refers to glycerol and fatty acids, which are structural components of lipids, not proteins. Choice D refers to glucose and fructose, which are carbohydrates. Pepsin aids in the digestion of proteins by severing the peptide bonds that join amino acids into long chains. Therefore, choice B is correct.

9. A: A good hypothesis is testable and logical, and can be used to predict future events. A good hypothesis is also simple, not complex.

10. C: Eukaryotes have nuclear membranes, but prokaryotes do not. Therefore, slides 1 and 3 are slides of eukaryotes, and slide 2 is a slide of a prokaryote.

11. C: All of the plants survived in the neutral soil, which was the soil with a pH of 7. As the acidity increased, fewer plants survived. Therefore, the correct answer is C.

12. C: DNA is a double helix, not a single helix. This eliminates choices A and B. DNA consists of the bases adenine, thymine, guanine, and cytosine. In RNA, uracil is substituted for thymine. Therefore, the correct answer is C.

13. D: Bacteria have both DNA and RNA. Most bacteria have a single, circular strand of DNA and short segments of DNA in plasmids. Therefore, choice D is correct.

14. C: Transcription is the process whereby a cell copies DNA onto RNA. DNA is not copied from one molecule to another, and is not copied from RNA to DNA.

15. A: Choice B discusses the construction of proteins, and choices C and D are both types of mutations. The first step of gene expression is transcription. Therefore, choice A is correct.

16. C: All of the choices listed are types of mutations or chromosomal changes. Substitution occurs when a nucleotide is replaced by a different nucleotide. Translocation occurs when two nonhomologous chromosomes exchange information. Deletion occurs when a piece of a chromosome breaks off and is omitted. Inversion occurs when a piece of a chromosome breaks off and reattaches in such a way that the order of the genes is reversed.

17. C: When a pure tall plant is crossed with a hybrid tall plant, 50% of the offspring will be hybrid tall plants. The missing combination combines a T gamete and a t gamete, resulting in a genotype of Tt. This plant will be a hybrid tall plant. Therefore, the correct answer is C.

18. B: Meiosis produces daughter cells with half the number of chromosomes as the parent cell. One half of 88 is 44. Therefore, the correct answer is B.

19. C: According to the Punnett square below, the probability that the offspring of a heterozygous, black-haired male and a white-haired female will have white hair (bb) is 50%.

	B	**b**
b	Bb	bb
b	Bb	bb

20. A: If red and white are incompletely dominant, then they will both be expressed, and the offspring will exhibit a third phenotype that is a blend of red and white. When red and white blend, pink is produced.

21. A: The cell replicates its DNA during interphase. The nucleolus is dismantled during prophase. The chromatids move to opposite ends of the cell during anaphase. This eliminates choices B, C, and D. The cell's chromosomes line up along the equatorial plane during metaphase.

22. C: Smooth muscle cells are elongated and spindle shaped. Cardiac muscle cells are cross-striated and quadrangular. Epithelial cells are tightly packed and cuboidal. This eliminates choices A, B, and D. Skeletal muscle cells are striated, cylindrical fibers with nuclei located towards the outer edges of the fibers.

23. B: Mammals of different species have similar body structures because they share a common ancestor. Common food sources, common environments, and similar reproductive processes would not result in similar skeletal structures. Therefore, the correct answer is B.

24. A: Both the red-shafted and yellow-shafted birds are Northern Flickers, so they share a common ancestor. Different environments and food sources would not cause the color differences seen in the two populations. Natural selection explains the differences in color. Each color is better suited for a specific environment, and individuals with the "right" color were the ones that survived long enough to reproduce. Therefore, the correct answer is A.

25. B: Gradualism states that evolution occurs slowly, with organisms exhibiting small changes over long periods of time. According to gradualism, the fossil record should show gradual changes over time. Punctuated equilibrium states that evolution occurs in spurts of sudden change. According to punctuated equilibrium, the fossil record should have large gaps. Therefore, the correct answer is B.

26. D: The seven categories of Linneaus's system, from broadest to narrowest, are kingdom, phylum, class, order, family, genus, and species. Of the choices given, class is the broadest category. Therefore, the correct answer is D.

27. A: Plants have more than one cell and can make their own food. Therefore, the correct answer is A.

28. B: Of the pairs given, only Gila monsters and clams belong to the same kingdom. Therefore, the correct answer is B.

29. C: Most fungi are multicellular. This eliminates choices A and D. Fungi range in size, from microscopic to macroscopic. This eliminates choice B. Also, many—but not all—fungi are decomposers. Fungi are heterotrophs that use spores to reproduce. Therefore, choice C is correct.

30. C: The Bacteria and Archaea kingdoms contains prokaryotes. The Protista and Fungi kingdoms contain eukaryotes. Therefore, the correct answer is C.

31. D: The prefix "homo" means same. The prefix "hetero" means different. The terms homogeneous and heterogeneous are used in chemistry to refer to solutions. The term heterologous means "of different origin." The term homologous refers to things that have a common origin. Therefore, the correct answer is D.

32. C: Firmicutes and euryarchaeota are not even in the same domain. Insects and slime molds are not even in the same kingdom. Red algae and baker's yeast are not in the same kingdom. Monocots and dicots are in the same kingdom. Therefore, the correct answer is C.

33. B: The only reactant containing carbon in the net equation for photosynthesis is carbon dioxide. Plants receive carbon dioxide primarily from the air that is taken in through the stomata in the epidermis. Therefore, choice B is correct.

34. A: Enzymes are large protein molecules that act as biological catalysts and play an important role in all bodily processes. They are not fat soluble, are not acids, and are not lipids. Therefore, choice A is correct.

35. C: Nutrients are not usable until they have been transported to the mitochondria for processing. Therefore, choice C is correct.

36. C: Energy pyramids show the total energy flow in an ecosystem. Number pyramids indicate the number of each type of organism in an ecosystem. Biomass pyramids indicate the total mass of living organisms in a specified area. Biomass pyramids can be inverted. For example, aquatic biomass pyramids are inverted due to the large number of zooplankton that feed on a smaller number of phytoplankton, which reproduce very quickly. Therefore, the correct answer is C.

37. A: The fat stored in a camel's hump helps it survive without food and water. The patches on a camel's knees protect them from being burned on the hot sand. A camel's thick fur and under wool provide warmth at night and insulation during the day. Two rows of eyelashes protect a camel's eyes from blowing sand.

38. D: Atoms make up molecules, which make up cells, which make up tissues, which make up organs, which make up systems. Therefore, choice D is correct.

39. C: When sodium bicarbonate was added to the test tube, the average number of bubbles counted by the students was 252. When sodium bicarbonate was not added to the test tube, that number was 190. These results indicate that the rate of photosynthesis increased as the concentration of carbon dioxide increased. Therefore, the correct answer is C.

40. A: Photosynthesis consists of light-dependent reactions and light-independent reactions. Water may be produced during oxygenic photosynthesis. Water does enter the plant through root hairs in the soil, and carbon dioxide enters the plant through stomata in the leaves and stems. Therefore, the correct answer is A.

41. B: Water and carbon dioxide are needed for photosynthesis. Xylem carries these reactants from the roots up to the leaves. Glucose is a product of photosynthesis, and is carried to the rest of the plant by phloem. Therefore, choice B is correct.

42. D: Placing the bag over the plant will not allow the student to determine whether the plant is producing glucose during photosynthesis. It will not affect the color of the light that is available to the plant. It will not affect the amount of water the plant absorbs through its roots. This eliminates choices A, B, and C. Water vapor produced as a result of transpiration should collect on the bag. Therefore, choice D is correct.

43. D: Thigmatropism is a response to touch. Phototropism is a response to light. Hydrotropism is a response to water. Gravitropism is a response to gravity, and the fact that the student placed some seedlings on their sides and some with their tops pointing either up or down suggests that this tropism is the one the student might be trying to investigate. Therefore, the correct answer is D.

44. B: Abiotic factors are nonliving factors. Producers, decomposers, and autotrophs are all organisms. This eliminates choices A, C, and D. Therefore, choice B, which lists nonliving factors only, is correct.

45. C: Phytoplankton are the first link in almost every marine food chain, and act as producers. Diatoms, which are shown in the figure, are yellow algae. Algae are classified as phytoplankton. The correct answer is C.

46. D: Organisms in the climax stage are typically larger, have longer life spans, and have more complex life cycles than organisms in the pioneer stage. They also typically have lower metabolic rates. This eliminates choices A, B, and C. Therefore, the correct answer is D.

47. A: Neutralism occurs when two organisms have no direct relationship to each other. Competition occurs when two organisms inhibit each other because they depend on the same resource. Amensalism occurs when one organism inhibits another organism, but remains unaffected by that organism. This eliminates choices B, C, and D. Mutualism is a type of symbiosis, and occurs when both organisms need each other to survive. This is the type of relationship that exists between termites and the protozoans that live in the digestive tracts of termites. Therefore, the correct answer is A.

48. C: All of the choices describe adaptations that help dolphins thrive in their marine environment. However, only choice C discusses oxygen conservation, which helps dolphins make long dives.

49. D: In an ecosystem, energy flows from a producer, to a primary consumer, to a secondary consumer, and then to a tertiary consumer. Choices A and B do not start with producers. Choice C is incorrect because the mountain lion and the hawk are not connected in the illustration of the food web provided.

50. B: Carnivores do not produce their own food, eat producers, or break down dead organic material. Carnivores are meat eaters, and can be secondary or even tertiary consumers. Therefore, the correct answer is B.

51. B: Decomposers break down organic matter. They do not convert nitrogen. This eliminates choice A. Denitrifying bacteria return nitrogen to the atmosphere. This eliminates choice C. Atmospheric nitrogen does not exist in a form organisms can use. This eliminates choice D. Nitrogen-fixing bacteria convert atmospheric nitrogen into nitrates that organisms can use. Therefore, the correct answer is B.

52. B: The levels of organization into which Earth's organisms can be arranged, from broadest to narrowest, are biosphere, ecosystem, community, population, and species. Therefore, the correct answer is B.

53. D: Since krill do not make their own food, they are not producers. Since krill do not eat primary consumers or secondary consumers, they are not secondary consumers or tertiary consumers. Since krill eat producers, they are primary consumers. Therefore, the correct answer is D.

54. D: Energy in an ecosystem comes from the sun. Organisms can store this energy as fats, sugars, and starches. The amount of energy in an ecosystem decreases with each trophic level. Energy does not increase in an ecosystem as it moves through each step of a food chain. Therefore, the correct answer is D.

Practice Test #2

1. During a laboratory investigation, biology students were asked to classify organisms on prepared slides as either eukaryotes or prokaryotes. Which of the following features should the students be able to observe in BOTH types of cells?

a. ribosomes
b. mitochondria
c. nucleus
d. Golgi apparatus

2. The euglena, shown in the image below, is a unicellular organism often found in ponds and puddles that must maintain homeostasis to survive. The euglena's environment can be described as a hypotonic solution.

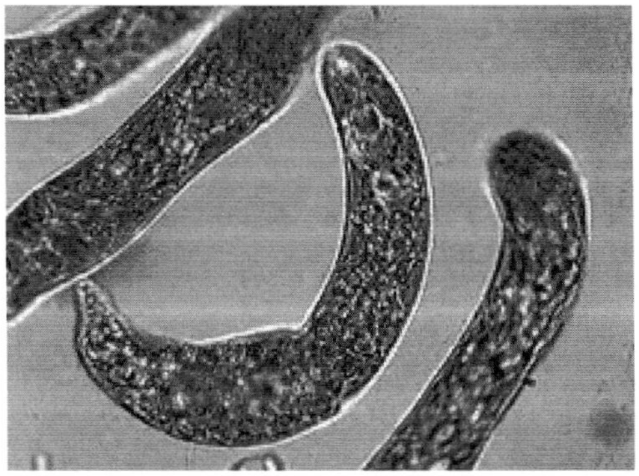

Which of the following BEST describes the mechanism used by the euglena to prevent bursting?

a. The stiff pellicle prevents water from diffusing through the cell membrane.
b. The motion of the flagellum prevents water from diffusing through the cell membrane.
c. The chloroplasts continually consume water, which prevents the cell from bursting.
d. The contractile vacuole excretes water out of the cell to prevent the cell from bursting.

3. In 1982, HIV was identified when it was observed that certain patients' immune systems were not fighting infections. Once this virus enters the body, it attacks lymphocytes. The image below is a scanning electron micrograph showing HIV budding from a lymphocyte.

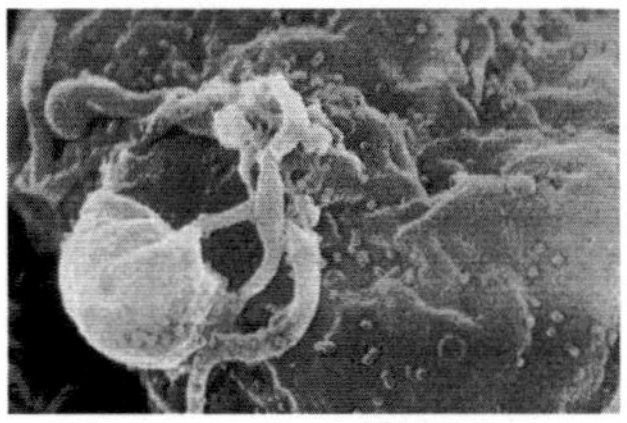

Which of the following is NOT true of the reproduction process of the HIV virus?

a. When the reproduction process is complete, new HIV particles leave the host cell to infect other cells.
b. The HIV virus has its own ribosomes, which it forces the host cell to utilize.
c. The HIV virus needs a host cell in order to reproduce or replicate.
d. The HIV virus's single-stranded RNA must be converted to double-stranded DNA.

4. The diagram below shows the various stages of the cell cycle in onion root tip cells.

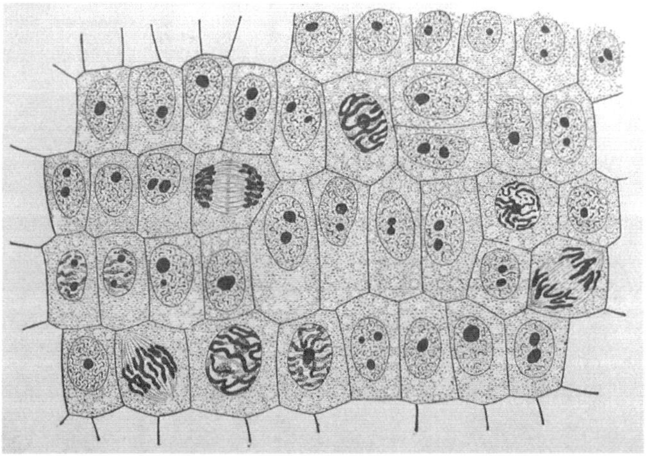

MOST of the plant cells in this diagram are in which of the following stages of the cell cycle?

a. telophase
b. prophase
c. anaphase
d. interphase

5. The diagram below shows the structure of a leaf.

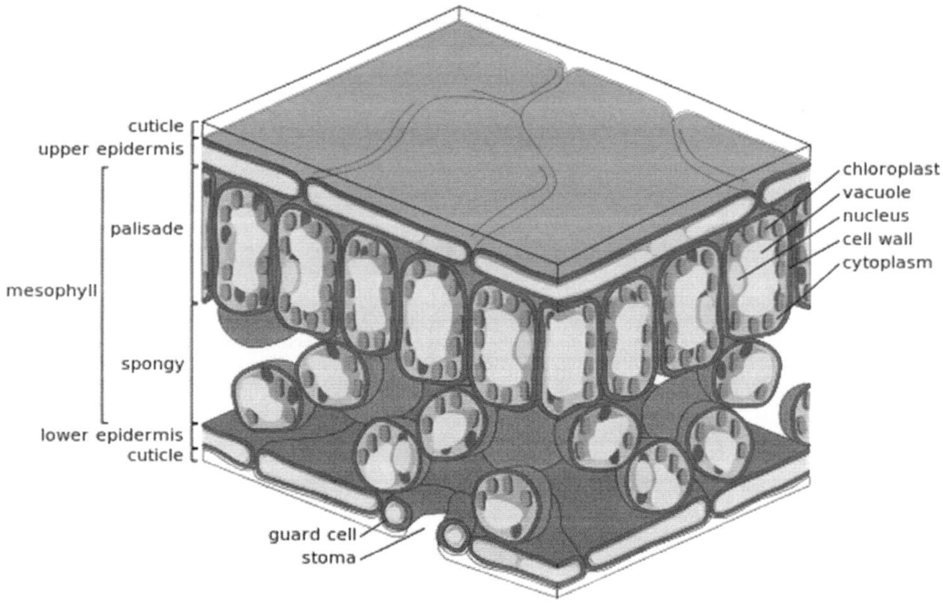

Which of the following BEST describes the function of the guard cells shown in the diagram?

a. They reduce water loss due to evaporation by trapping water vapor near the plant's surface.
b. They conduct water and dissolved minerals from the roots.
c. They open and close pores to allow for the exchange of gases between the atmosphere and the leaf.
d. They are full of chloroplasts, and are located where photosynthesis mainly takes place.

6. Scientists must be able to recognize limitations to science to conduct effective research. Which of the following is NOT a limitation of science?

a. Scientific experiments can be fully controlled.
b. Science cannot answer questions about values or morality.
c. Scientific observations may be faulty.
d. Science must deal with testable, repeatable phenomena.

7. Cells must maintain homeostasis to survive. One method cells use to ensure a stable internal environment is facilitated diffusion. Which of the following is NOT true of facilitated diffusion?

a. Facilitated diffusion is a type of passive transport.
b. Facilitated diffusion occurs down a concentration gradient.
c. Facilitated diffusion is slower than simple diffusion.
d. Facilitated diffusion does not require extra energy.

8. The diagram below shows the structural formula for lactose. Lactose, a compound of two simple sugars, is the type of sugar found in milk. About 40 million Americans are lactose intolerant, meaning they are unable to digest this milk sugar. People who suffer from lactose intolerance do not produce enough of the protein lactase.

Lactose

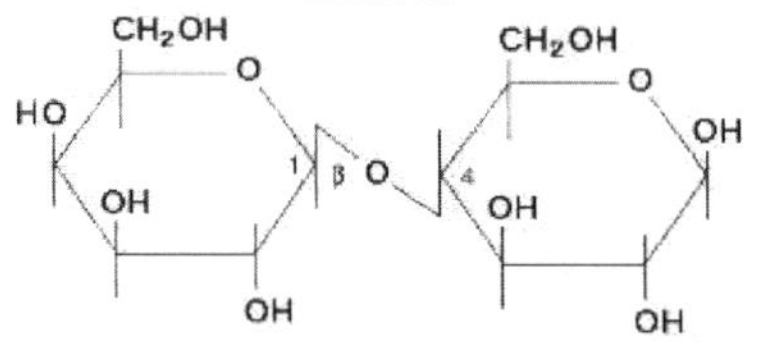

Which of the following statements is MOST LIKELY true about the biomolecule lactase?

a. Lactase is a steroid that regulates metabolism.
b. Lactase is a hormone that sends a signal to the digestive system to secrete digestive juices.
c. Lactase is an antibody that acts as a catalyst in the digestive process of lactose.
d. Lactase is an enzyme that acts as a catalyst in the digestive process of lactose.

9. A biology student examines a prepared slide of blood under a microscope. He observes two types of cells, and documents his observations in the following table.

Cells	Color	Nucleus	Number	Size
Type 1	pink with a huge, dark purple center	Yes	3	approximately twice as large as type 2
Type 2	pink with a dark edge	No	677	smaller than type 1

Which of the following is a reasonable assumption based on the student's observations?

a. Both the type 1 and type 2 cells are red blood cells.
b. Both the type 1 and type 2 cells are white blood cells.
c. The type 1 cells are white blood cells, and the type 2 cells are red blood cells.
d. The type 1 cells are red blood cells, and the type 2 cells are white blood cells.

10. An animal cell is shown in the figure below.

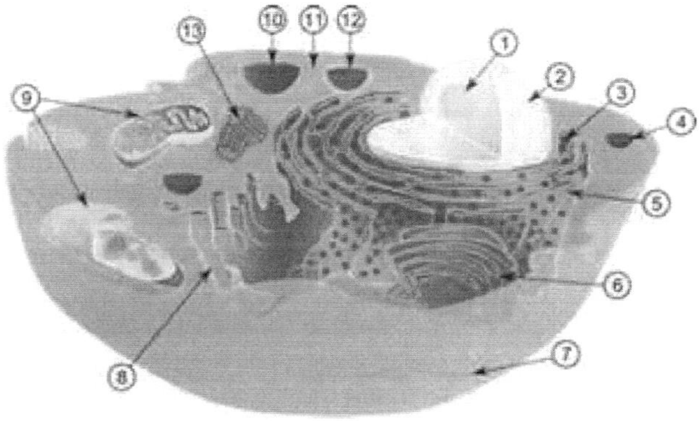

In which of the following structures does protein synthesis occur?

a. 3
b. 7
c. 9
d. 11

11. A biology student is studying the effects of acid rain on tomato plants. He plants four tomato plants in identical pots, using the same type of soil to fill each pot. He places the pots together in the same location. They receive the same amount of sunlight and water each day. The only difference is the pH of the water used to water the plants. The first plant receives water with a neutral pH of 7, which will allow the student to better determine the effects of giving plants water that is more acidic. The second plant receives water with a pH of 5. The third receives water with a pH of 3. The fourth receives water with a pH of 1. Which of the following is a serious flaw in the design of this experiment?

a. The experiment has only one independent variable.
b. The experiment has several constants.
c. The experiment has no repetition.
d. The experiment has no control.

12. Genetic information is contained in deoxyribonucleic acid (DNA) molecules, which are primarily located in the nuclei of most organisms. Each DNA molecule has a double helix shape, and consists of two strands connected by base pairs at regular intervals. Which of the following BEST describes how bases are paired in DNA molecules?

a. Adenine always pairs with thymine, and guanine always pairs with cytosine.
b. Adenine always pairs with guanine, and thymine always pairs with cytosine.
c. Adenine always pairs with uracil, and guanine always pairs with cytosine.
d. Adenine always pairs with guanine, and uracil always pairs with cytosine.

13. Organisms are classified as eukaryotes or prokaryotes based on their basic body structure. Which of the following is true of organisms and the type of genetic information they contain?

a. Both eukaryotes and prokaryotes contain DNA enclosed in membrane-bound nuclei.
b. Both eukaryotes and prokaryotes contain DNA, but prokaryotes typically only have a single, circular chromosome.
c. All eukaryotes and most prokaryotes contain DNA, but Archaebacteria only contain RNA.
d. All eukaryotes contain DNA, and all prokaryotes contain only RNA.

14. In order to survive, cells must be able to synthesize molecules from their DNA templates. Which of the following BEST describes the process of translation?

a. During translation, amino acids are joined together in chains to form complex carbohydrates.
b. During translation, amino acids are joined together in chains to form proteins.
c. During translation, sugars are joined together in chains to form complex carbohydrates.
d. During translation, sugars are joined together in chains to form proteins.

15. Which of the following occurs during the phase of mitosis known as telophase?

a. A nucleus forms in each daughter cell.
b. The centrioles move to opposite ends of the cell.
c. The cell's DNA is replicated.
d. The chromosomes attach to the spindle apparatus.

16. Mutations refer to changes in an organism's DNA. One type of mutation is translocation, which occurs during meiosis. Which of the following BEST describes translocation?

a. Two nonhomologous chromosomes exchange genetic information.
b. Two homologous chromosomes exchange genetic information.
c. A segment of a chromosome breaks off and reattaches at the same position, but the order of the genes is reversed.
d. A segment of a chromosome breaks off, and does not reattach.

17. A genetics student performs the same experiment completed by Gregor Mendel with pea plants. The Punnett square below shows the possible genetic combinations when she crosses two pea plants that are heterozygous for the gene associated with round seeds (Rr).

	R	**r**
R	RR	Rr
r	Rr	??

Which of the following correctly completes the square?

a. Rr
b. rR
c. rr
d. RR

18. Both living species of elephants, the African elephant and the Asian elephant, have 56 chromosomes in their body cells. If one of these cells undergoes meiosis, how many chromosomes will each of the daughter cells have?

a. 7
b. 14
c. 28
d. 56

19. DNA fingerprinting was first developed in England in 1985 by Sir Alec Jeffreys. Since that time, DNA fingerprinting has been used for paternity testing. It has also been used to identify victims of crime and to convict criminals. Which of the following BEST describes the technique of DNA fingerprinting?

a. DNA fingerprinting compares stem cells from different individuals.
b. DNA fingerprinting compares entire DNA molecules from different individuals.
c. DNA fingerprinting compares segments of DNA molecules from different individuals.
d. DNA fingerprinting compares specific amino acids from different individuals.

20. In horses, black hair is dominant, and light-colored hair is recessive. If a white stallion is crossed with a mare that is homozygous for the gene for black hair, what is the probability that ALL of the offspring will have black hair?

a. 100%
b. 50%
c. 25%
d. 0%

21. A biology student prepared the following chart listing the four major types of biomolecules and their functions.

Type of Biomolecule	Major Function(s)
1	short-term energy storage; intermediate-term energy storage
2	form structures; regulation
3	form cell membranes; long-term energy storage
4	store information

Which of the following correctly identifies the biomolecules described in the chart, from 1 to 4?

a. carbohydrates, lipids, proteins, and nucleic acids
b. carbohydrates, proteins, lipids, and nucleic acids
c. lipids, proteins, carbohydrates, and nucleic acids
d. nucleic acids, proteins, carbohydrates, and lipids

22. The flowering plant known as the snapdragon produces white, yellow, and crimson flowers. When a snapdragon that is homozygous for the gene for white flowers is crossed with a crimson snapdragon that is homozygous for the gene for crimson flowers, heterozygous offspring with pink flowers are produced. Which of the following terms correctly describes this phenomenon?

a. Mendelian inheritance
b. polygenic inheritance
c. pleiotropy
d. incomplete dominance

23. The figure below shows the forelimbs of various mammals. Which of the following BEST explains why the similar forelimbs shown below are considered homologous structures?

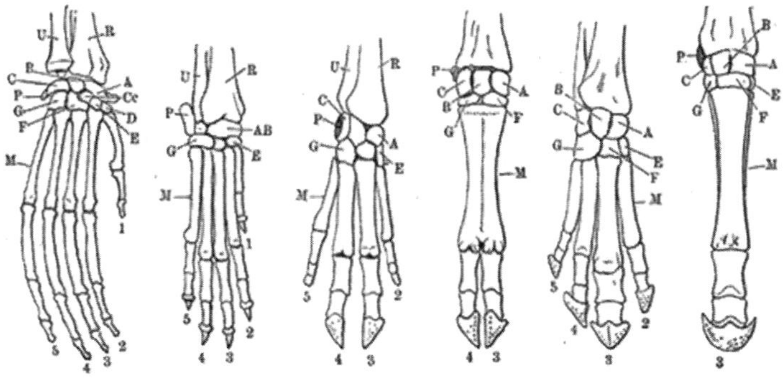

a. They are all forelimbs.
b. They have similar structures.
c. They have a common underlying anatomy that was also seen in their last common ancestor.
d. They evolved from a common ancestor, as did all other vertebrates.

24. Punctuated equilibrium and gradualism are both models for evolutionary change, but they are very different theories. Which of the following statements is true of the evolutionary theory known as gradualism?

a. Several closely related species from isolated populations evolve rapidly.
b. Fossils showing intermediate changes will not necessarily be found.
c. Evolution occurs in spurts of rapid change.
d. Speciation occurs gradually.

25. Rat snakes are constrictors found throughout much of the Northern Hemisphere, and they live in all types of terrains. Rat snakes can be a wide variety of colors, including black, orange, and green. Some also have yellow stripes. Which of the following BEST explains the role of natural selection in the development of these different colors?

a. Rat snakes developed different colors because they relied on different foods for survival.
b. Rat snakes that were different colors survived in different locations because they were best suited to specific environments.
c. Rat snakes that were a specific color killed off the snakes that were different colors.
d. Rat snakes that were a specific color only mated with snakes of the same color.

26. In 1753, a Swedish botanist named Carolus Linnaeus (pictured below) developed a scientific binomial naming system that is still used today.

According to the naming system developed by Linnaeus, which of the following is the MOST SPECIFIC category of classification?

a. phylum
b. order
c. family
d. class

27. Many modern biologists use a six kingdom system to classify organisms. These six kingdoms are Animalia, Plantae, Fungi, Protista, Archaea, and Bacteria. Which of the following is true of organisms that are part of Kingdom Animalia (animals)?

a. They are multicellular and autotrophic.
b. They are multicellular and heterotrophic.
c. They are unicellular and autotrophic.
d. They are unicellular and heterotrophic.

28. According to modern taxonomic classification, which of the following organisms are MOST CLOSELY related?

a. ferns and lichens
b. apes and squids
c. bacteria and algae
d. conifers and mushrooms

29. When the six kingdom classification system is used, many eukaryotes are classed as members of Kingdom Protista. Which of the following BEST describes organisms that are part of Kingdom Protista (protists)?

a. All protists are microscopic and unicellular.
b. All protists are macroscopic and multicellular.
c. All protists are microscopic and autotrophic.
d. Protists may be unicellular and microscopic, or may be multicellular and macroscopic.

30. Which of the following correctly arranges the categories that comprise the modern classification system used today from most inclusive to least inclusive?

a. domain, kingdom, phylum, order, class, family, genus, and species
b. kingdom, domain, phylum, order, class, family, genus, and species
c. domain, kingdom, phylum, class, order, family, genus, and species
d. species, genus, family, order, class, phylum, kingdom, and domain

31. Species is one of the seven categories that comprise the classification system devised by Carolus Linnaeus, who is now considered the father of taxonomy. Which of the following is NOT true of the category known as species?

a. Species is the major subdivision of the genus category.
b. Members of the same species typically have many common characteristics.
c. Species are non-changing, and can never split into additional groups.
d. Members of a species are able to breed and produce viable, fertile offspring.

32. Food chains consist of many different types of organisms. Which of the following organisms could be categorized as primary consumers?

a. tapeworms
b. toadstools
c. plant parasites
d. lions

33. The rate of photosynthesis in green plants is affected by several factors. Two of these factors are represented in the graph below.

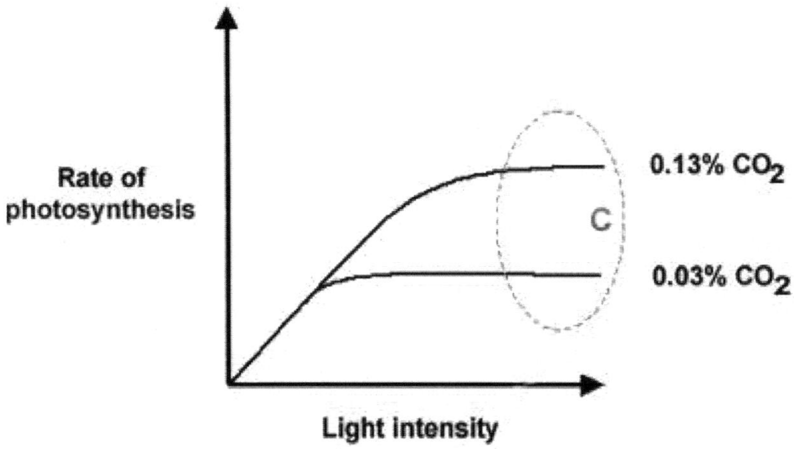

Which of the following statements correctly interprets the information presented in the area labeled "C"?

a. The rate of photosynthesis is unaffected by CO2 concentration.
b. The rate of photosynthesis increases as the concentration of CO2 increases.
c. The rate of photosynthesis increases as light intensity increases.
d. The rate of photosynthesis is unaffected by light intensity.

34. A potential energy diagram showing the effect of an enzyme on a biological reaction is shown below.

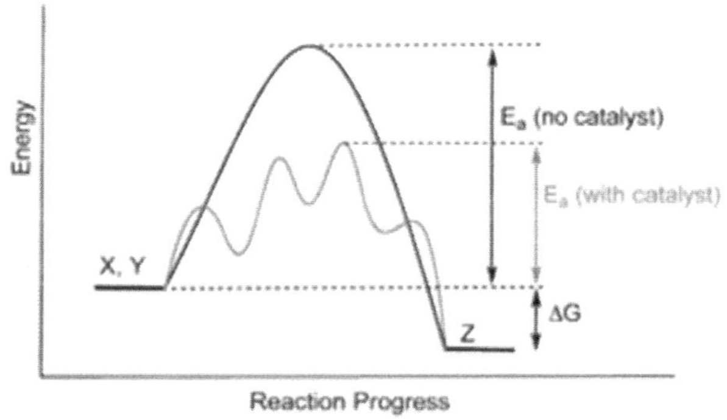

Which of the following BEST describes the role of enzymes in biological reactions?

a. Enzymes are biological catalysts that lower the potential energy of the reactants in a biological reaction.
b. Enzymes are biological catalysts that lower the required activation energy for biological reactions.
c. Enzymes are biological catalysts that lower the potential energy of the products of a biological reaction.
d. Enzymes are biological catalysts that are consumed during biological reactions.

35. In mammals, blood pH must be kept fairly constant (very close to 7.4) in order for these animals to survive. Which two organs play the MOST IMPORTANT role in regulating blood pH in mammals?

a. kidneys and lungs
b. heart and lungs
c. kidneys and liver
d. liver and lungs

36. Yaks are especially well suited to their natural environment in the Himalayas. Which of the following adaptations is MOST helpful in allowing yaks to deal with the low oxygen content in their mountain environment?

a. thick fur
b. small number of sweat glands
c. broad hooves
d. large lungs

37. All heterotrophs use cellular respiration to obtain the energy needed to survive. Which of the following statements about cellular respiration is true?

a. Energy released during cellular respiration is stored as ATP.
b. Energy released during cellular respiration is stored as NADPH.
c. Glucose produced during cellular respiration is stored as glycogen.
d. Glucose produced during cellular respiration is stored as starch.

38. Vascular tissue in plants is responsible for the upward movement of water and minerals from the root hairs to the rest of the plant. Which of the following is NOT partially responsible for the upward movement of material in vascular tissue?

a. adhesion
b. cohesion
c. Brownian motion
d. capillary action

39. During a laboratory investigation, students examined live *Elodea* submerged in a test tube of pond water to determine the effect of the distance from a light source on the rate of photosynthesis. The rate of photosynthesis was measured by determining the number of bubbles produced in a 30-second period. The results were then recorded in the table below.

Distance (cm)	Number of bubbles produced in 30 seconds
10	94
20	69
30	59
40	56
50	50

Which of the following can be inferred based on the results shown in the data table?

a. The rate of photosynthesis increases exponentially as the distance from the light source increases.
b. The rate of photosynthesis is unaffected by the distance from the light source.
c. The rate of photosynthesis increases as the distance from the light source increases.
d. The rate of photosynthesis decreases as the distance from the light source increases.

40. Photosynthesis is a process whereby energy from the sun is converted to a form plants can use. Which of the following lists two reactants that are needed for photosynthesis to occur?

a. water and glucose
b. water and carbon dioxide
c. oxygen and glucose
d. oxygen and carbon dioxide

41. Angiosperms are flowering plants that use seeds to reproduce. Which choice lists the processes associated with angiosperm reproduction in the order in which they occur?

a. pollination, fertilization, seed formation, and seed dispersal
b. fertilization, pollination, seed formation, and seed dispersal
c. pollination, seed formation, fertilization, and seed dispersal
d. pollination, seed dispersal, seed formation, and fertilization

42. A biology student places one end of a stalk of celery into a beaker containing a solution of red food coloring for several hours. When she removes the celery from the beaker, she notices that parts of the celery are now red. Which of the following BEST explains why this occurred?

a. The red food coloring moved through the stomata as a result of osmosis.
b. The red food coloring moved up the root hairs as a result of capillary action.
c. The red food coloring moved up the phloem as a result of capillary action.
d. The red food coloring moved up the xylem as a result of capillary action.

43. A biology student is investigating tropisms in plants. The student observes the response of the roots of radish seedlings to a light source placed to the right of the roots. All of the roots grow away from the light source. Which of the following tropisms is the student MOST LIKELY investigating?

a. gravitropism
b. thigmotropism
c. hydrotropism
d. phototropism

44. Environmental factors that affect organisms are classified as either abiotic or biotic. Which of the following lists ONLY abiotic factors that can affect organisms?

a. humidity, amount of carbon dioxide, and soil density
b. temperature, types of bacteria, and soil pH
c. amount of oxygen, soil salinity, and types of heterotrophs
d. soil nitrogen content, amount of sunlight, and types of decomposers

45. Decomposers, which include bacteria, fungi, and various other microorganisms, make up a special category of consumers in an ecosystem. Which of the following BEST describes the role of decomposers in an ecosystem?

a. Decomposers are autotrophs that convert sunlight into sugars needed by other organisms.
b. Decomposers produce over half of the needed oxygen for an ecosystem.
c. Decomposers play a vital role in breaking down plant and animal material to release nutrients needed for healthy soils.
d. Decomposers fix nitrogen from the atmosphere into a form that other organisms in an ecosystem can use.

46. A gradual change in an ecosystem over a period of time is known as ecological succession. The figure below shows the ecological succession of vegetation in a temperate deciduous forest after a natural disaster such as a forest fire.

Based on the figure above, which of the following is the BEST description of ecological succession?

a. Succession is a rapid process, and all stages of development occur simultaneously.
b. Succession is a rapid, ordered progression.
c. Succession is a gradual, ordered progression.
d. Succession is a gradual, random process.

47. Many different relationships exist between organisms that are part of an ecosystem. For example, an interesting relationship exists between an African bird and rhinos. The birds follow the rhinos and eat the insects that the rhinos disturb as they amble along. The birds are helped, but the rhinos are neither helped nor harmed by this relationship. Which of the following terms BEST describes this relationship?

a. commensalism
b. mutualism
c. parasitism
d. amensalism

48. All organisms on Earth can be arranged into five levels of organization. Which of the following correctly organizes these levels from most exclusive to least exclusive?

a. biosphere, ecosystem, population, community, and species
b. species, population, community, ecosystem, and biosphere
c. biosphere, ecosystem, community, population, and species
d. species, community, population, ecosystem, and biosphere

49. A marine food web for an ecosystem in Alaska is illustrated below.

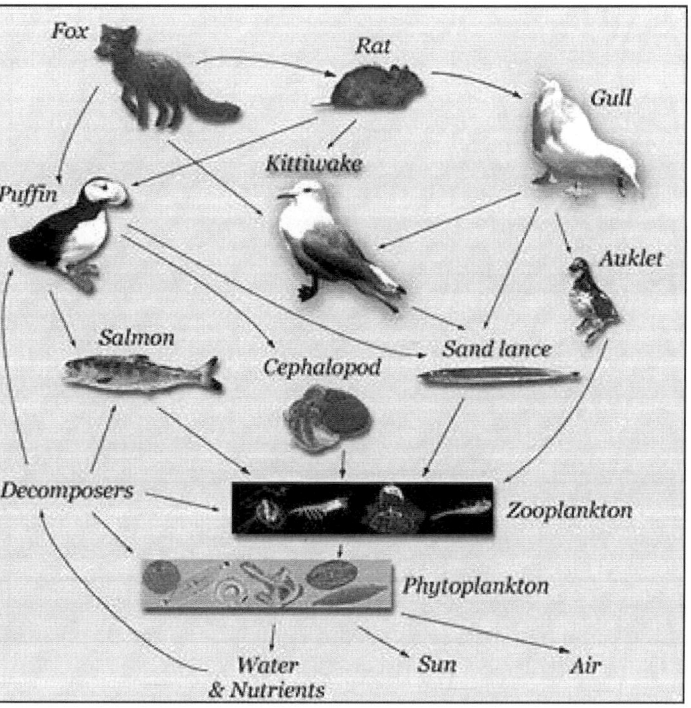

Which of the following describes how energy might flow through this food web?

a. fox → gull → auklet → zooplankton → phytoplankton
b. phytoplankton → zooplankton → kittiwake → rat → fox
c. fox → kittiwake → sand lance → zooplankton → phytoplankton
d. phytoplankton → zooplankton → cephalopod → puffin → fox

50. Information about an ecosystem can be represented using several types of pyramids. Which of the following pyramids can NEVER be inverted?

a. biomass pyramids
b. number pyramids
c. both biomass pyramids and number pyramids
d. energy pyramids

51. Many types of symbiosis exist in nature. Which of the following is NOT an example of symbiosis?

a. predation
b. mutualism
c. parasitism
d. commensalism

52. Environmental changes such as climate changes can greatly impact an ecosystem. Which of the following is NOT an example of how climate changes could impact ecosystems?

a. Warming could force species to migrate to higher latitudes and altitudes.
b. Warming could lead to birds migrating and nesting earlier.
c. Warming could lead to a loss of sea ice as a habitat for particular species.
d. Warming could increase a species' resistance to disease.

53. The kangaroo rat has many adaptations that allow it to survive in its harsh desert environment.

Which of the following adaptations does NOT help the kangaroo rat escape from predators?

a. the ability to obtain needed water from seeds
b. excellent hearing
c. large back legs
d. sandy fur color

54. Grasshoppers are insects that are members of the order *Orthoptera*. Grasshoppers play an important role in this food web, as they are a food source for birds.

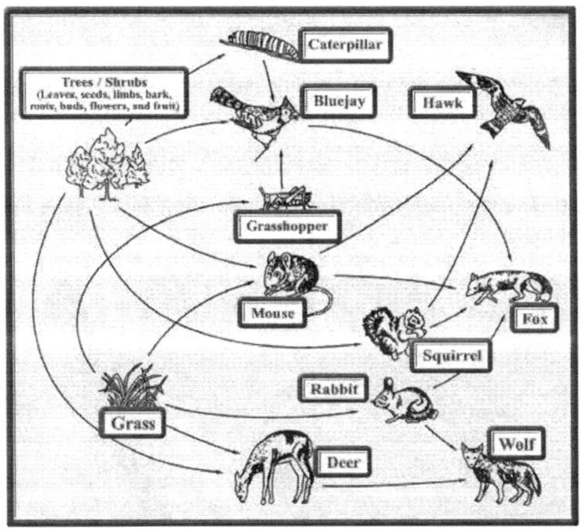

Which of the following terms BEST describes the role of grasshoppers in this food web?

a. producers
b. predators
c. carnivores
d. herbivores

Answer Key and Explanations for Test #2

1. A: Prokaryotic cells lack a nucleus and membrane-bound organelles such as mitochondria and Golgi complexes. This eliminates choices B, C, and D. Both prokaryotic cells and eukaryotic cells contain ribosomes. Therefore, choice A is correct.

2. D: The euglena's pellicle is not very stiff, and does not prevent water from entering the cell. The motion of the flagellum has no effect on the diffusion of water through the cell membrane. The water consumed during photosynthesis by the chloroplasts would never be enough to prevent the cell from bursting. This eliminates choices A, B, and C. The contractile vacuole excretes excess water from the cell. Without it, the cell would burst. Therefore, the correct answer is D.

3. B: The HIV virus cannot reproduce on its own. The virus enters a cell and converts its RNA into DNA, and then forces the machinery of the host cell to replicate this DNA. New HIV particles can leave the host cell to infect other cells. This means that choices A, C, and D are all true. Choice B is NOT true. The HIV virus does not have its own ribosomes, and uses the ribosomes of the host cell. Therefore, choice B is correct.

4. D: Cells spend most of their time in interphase. All of the cells in the diagram with a single, solid nucleus in the center are in interphase. Cells with nuclei that appear to be broken up are in prophase. Cells containing a connected spindle are in metaphase. Cells with broken spindles are in anaphase. Cells with two nuclei are in telophase. The correct answer is D.

5. C: Trichomes are hair-like cells that trap water to reduce evaporation. Xylem transports water and minerals upward from the roots of a plant to other parts of the plant. The parenchyma is full of chloroplasts, and is where photosynthesis mainly takes place. This eliminates choices A, B, and D. Guard cells open and close pores on the undersides of leaves that allow for the exchange of gases between the atmosphere and a plant's leaves. Therefore, choice C is correct.

6. A: Science cannot answer questions about value or morality, and must focus on testable and repeatable phenomena. Scientific observations may be faulty. A scientific experiment can never be fully controlled. Even if complete control were possible, this would not be a limitation of science, but rather a strength. Therefore, the correct choice is A.

7. C: Facilitated transport is considered a type of passive transport because it does not require extra energy. It also occurs down a concentration gradient. This eliminates choices A, B, and D. Facilitated transport is faster than simple diffusion. Therefore, the correct answer is C.

8. D: Lactase is a special protein molecule that is also an enzyme. Steroids and hormones are not proteins. This eliminates choices A and B. Antibodies are special proteins, but they do not aid in digestion. This eliminates choice C. Lactase is an enzyme that initiates the breakdown of the lactose biomolecule. Therefore, the correct choice is D.

9. C: Because stain was used to prepare these slides, color cannot be used to determine the cell type. Red blood cells are much more numerous than white blood cells, and are much smaller. White blood cells are less numerous and much larger than red blood cells. They also contain large nuclei that are easily observed. Therefore, the correct answer is C.

10. A: Ribosomes synthesize proteins. Proteins are not synthesized in the mitochondria, the cytoskeleton, or the cytoplasm. Therefore, the correct answer is A.

11. C: A good experiment has only one independent variable, several constants, and a control. This experiment has all of these. However, this experiment lacks repetition. The student should use a group of plants—not just one—to investigate the effect of each pH on plant growth. Therefore, the correct choice is C.

12. A: The four bases in DNA are adenine, thymine, guanine, and cytosine. Uracil replaces thymine in RNA. This eliminates choices C and D. In DNA, adenine pairs with thymine, and guanine pairs with cytosine. Therefore, the correct answer is A.

13. B: All eukaryotes and prokaryotes contain DNA and RNA. This eliminates choices C and D. Prokaryotes do not have membrane-bound nuclei. This eliminates choice A. Prokaryotes typically have a single, circular chromosome. They may have plasmids that contain small segments of DNA, but generally they only contain one circular chromosome. Therefore, the correct answer is B.

14. B: During the process of translation, ribosomes synthesize proteins from DNA templates. Proteins consist of numerous amino acids linked together. Choices A and D are incorrect because they do not reflect the fact that proteins are chains of amino acids. Choice C is incorrect because it does not correctly describe what occurs during translation. It discusses the formation of carbohydrates, not proteins.

15. A: The cell's DNA is replicated during interphase. The centrioles move to opposite ends of the cell during prophase. The chromosomes attach to the spindle during metaphase. This eliminates choices B, C, and D. A nucleus forms in each daughter cell during telophase. Therefore, the correct answer is A.

16. A: Choices C and D describe inversion and deletion, respectively. Choice B is incorrect because the exchange is not between two homologous chromosomes, but between two nonhomologous chromosomes. Therefore, the correct answer is A.

17. C: The Punnett square provided demonstrates the law of segregation. About 25% of the offspring of a hybrid cross will exhibit the recessive trait (in this case rr). Applying this fact or completing the Punnett square will both give the correct answer, which is C.

18. C: Meiosis results in the production of gametes. If the body cells of an elephant undergo meiosis, the daughter cells will contain 28 chromosomes. This is one half of the original number of chromosomes in the elephant's body cells (56). Therefore, the correct answer is C.

19. C: Most of our DNA is identical to everyone else's. DNA fingerprinting specifically targets short segments of DNA that are repeated many times in an individual. These short segments are different for each person, making them ideal for DNA fingerprinting. Therefore, choice C is correct.

20. A: The white stallion is homozygous for the gene for white hair, and the black mare is homozygous for the gene for black hair. All of their offspring will be heterozygous for the gene for black hair. Therefore, the correct choice is A.

21. B: Carbohydrates provide short-term and intermediate-term energy storage. Proteins form structures and provide regulation. Lipids form cell membranes and provide long-term energy storage. Nucleic acids store information. Therefore, the correct answer is B.

22. D: This cross is non-Mendelian because neither gene is dominant. This eliminates choice A. Pleiotropy involves several traits, and polygenic inheritance involves several genes. This eliminates choices B and C. Since the snapdragon that was homozygous for the gene for white flowers and the snapdragon that was homozygous for the gene for crimson flowers produced heterozygous offspring with pink flowers, the inheritance pattern seen in this plant is incomplete dominance. Therefore, the correct choice is D.

23. C: All of the diagrams are of forelimbs, all of the forelimbs have similar structures, and all of the forelimbs pictured are found in vertebrates, but none of these facts mean that these forelimbs are homologous structures. They are homologous structures because of their common underlying anatomy, which was also seen in their last common ancestor. Therefore, the correct answer is C.

24. D: Choices A, B, and C are all true statements regarding punctuated equilibrium, a theory which suggests that evolution can occur rapidly, and helps to explain gaps in the fossil record. Gradualism proposes that evolution occurs slowly. Therefore, choice D is correct.

25. B: According to the theory of natural selection, rat snakes (and other organisms) that are best suited to their environment will survive to reproduce. This would explain why rat snakes of different colors are found in different areas. Therefore, choice B is correct.

26. C: Linnaeus's system consists of seven categories: kingdom, phylum, class, order, family, genus, and species. Kingdom is the broadest category, and species is the most specific. However, of the choices given, family is the most specific. Therefore, the correct answer is C.

27. B: Animals consist of more than one cell, and they cannot make their own food. Therefore, the correct answer is B.

28. B: Of the pairs provided, only apes and squids are in the same kingdom. Therefore, the correct answer is B.

29. D: All eukaryotes that are not considered part of Kingdom Animalia, Kingdom Plantae, or Kingdom Fungi are classified as part of Kingdom Protista. This kingdom includes algae, protozoa, slime molds, and other organisms. Some are microscopic, and some are macroscopic. Some are unicellular, and some are multicellular. Therefore, choice D is correct.

30. C: From largest (most inclusive) to smallest (least inclusive), the categories that comprise the modern classification system used today are domain, kingdom, phylum, class, order, family, genus, and species. Therefore, the correct answer is C.

31. C: Choices A, B, and D are all true. Choice C is false. Species can split into additional groups. Speciation is the process whereby one species separates into two groups and a new species is formed. For example, geographic separation can cause speciation. Therefore, the correct answer is C.

32. C: Primary consumers eat producers. Tapeworms receive nourishment from consumers. Toadstools are decomposers. Lions are carnivores. Plant parasites rely on plants, which are producers, for survival. Therefore, the correct answer is C.

33. B: The portion labeled "C" is highlighting the difference in the rate of photosynthesis in green plants at two different CO_2 concentrations. The higher CO_2 concentration of 0.13% is associated with a faster rate of photosynthesis than the CO_2 concentration of 0.03% is. The graph shows that the rate of photosynthesis increases as CO_2 concentration increases. Therefore, the correct answer is B.

34. B: Enzymes do not affect the potential energy of reactants or products, and are not consumed during reactions. Enzymes do lower the required activation energy for biological reactions. Therefore, the correct answer is B.

35. A: Blood pH in mammals is chiefly regulated by the kidneys and lungs. The lungs remove nearly all of the CO_2 from the blood, preventing acidosis. Bicarbonate is adjusted by the kidneys to prevent acidosis and alkalosis. Therefore, the correct answer is A.

36. D: Thick fur and a small number of sweat glands are adaptations that allow organisms to cope with cold temperatures. The yak's broad hooves help it to navigate rough terrain. Large lungs help yaks deal with the low oxygen content in their environment. Therefore, the correct answer is D.

37. A: Cellular respiration is the process whereby energy is released from glucose and temporarily stored as ATP. NADPH is a compound produced during photosynthesis. Glucose is used during cellular respiration, not produced. Therefore, the correct answer is A.

38. C: Capillary action, which relies on several properties (including adhesion and cohesion), is responsible for the upward movement of water and minerals from a plant's roots to its leaves. Brownian motion is the movement of microscopic particles suspended in a liquid due to the motion of the liquid's molecules. It is not involved in the movement of water through a plant. Therefore, the correct answer is C.

39. D: The table shows that as the distance from the light source increases from 10 cm to 50 cm, the number of bubbles counted decreases. Therefore, the rate of photosynthesis decreases as the distance from the light source increases. The correct answer is D.

40. B: If light and chlorophyll are present, carbon dioxide and water will be converted into glucose and oxygen through photosynthesis. Therefore, the correct answer is B.

41. A: Flowers are pollinated and then fertilized. Then, seeds form, and the ovary ripens. Finally, the seeds are dispersed. Therefore, the correct answer is A.

42. D: Xylem is the vascular tissue that transports materials up a plant's stem. The red food coloring moved up the xylem as a result of capillary action. Therefore, the correct answer is D.

43. D: Gravitropism is a response to gravity. Thigmotropism is a response to touch. Hydrotropism is a response to water. Phototropism is a response to light, which is the tropism the student is most likely investigating. Therefore, the correct answer is D.

44. A: Abiotic factors are nonliving factors. Humidity, soil pH, amount of oxygen, amount of carbon dioxide, soil salinity, soil density, soil nitrogen content, and amount of sunlight are all examples of abiotic factors. However, bacteria, heterotrophs, and decomposers are all living things. This eliminates choices B, C, and D. Therefore, the correct choice is A.

45. C: Decomposers are heterotrophs that do not produce oxygen, fix nitrogen, or convert sunlight into sugars. This eliminates choices A, B, and D. Decomposers break down plant and animal material into smaller components, which releases the nutrients contained in this material. Therefore, the correct choice is C.

46. C: The time required for ecological succession to occur indicates that it is a gradual process, not a rapid one. This eliminates choices A and B. The fact that the diagram shows different plants reentering the ecosystem at different times indicates that succession is an orderly process, not a random one. This eliminates choice D. Therefore, the correct choice is C.

47. A: Mutualism occurs when organisms depend on each other to survive. Parasitism occurs when at least one organism is harmed. Amensalism occurs when at least one organism is inhibited. In the example given, the bird benefits, but the rhino is unaffected. This eliminates choices B, C, and D. Commensalism occurs when one organism benefits, and the other is unaffected. Therefore, the correct answer is A.

48. B: The biosphere, which is the most inclusive level, consists of ecosystems. Ecosystems consist of communities, which consist of populations, which consist of species. Species is the most exclusive level. Therefore, the correct answer is B.

49. D: The source of energy in a food web is a producer. Energy flows to a primary consumer, then to a secondary consumer, and then to a tertiary consumer, and so on. Choices A and C do not start with producers. Choice B is incorrect because the zooplankton and the kittiwake are not directly connected in this food web (the kittiwake does not eat zooplankton). Therefore, the correct choice is D.

50. D: Biomass pyramids and number pyramids can be inverted in some situations. For example, a number pyramid for a single tree that provides food for thousands of ants would be inverted. Energy pyramids can never be inverted. Energy always decreases as it moves through an ecosystem. Therefore, the correct answer is D.

51. A: Mutualism, parasitism, and commensalism all refer to close relationships between two different species that persist over a period of time. All three relationships are considered types of symbiosis. Predation is the relationship between predator and prey. Therefore, the correct answer is A.

52. D: Climate changes such as warming can lead to species being forced to leave an area; to birds migrating and nesting earlier, and possibly being unable to obtain their required food sources; and to a loss of sea ice, resulting in a loss of habitat. Therefore choices A, B, and C are all possible effects of climate change, and can be eliminated. Climate change typically supports the spread of pathogens and disease, and does not increase a species' resistance to disease. Therefore, the correct choice is D.

53. A: A kangaroo rat's excellent hearing allows it to hear predators such as owls. Its large back legs allow it to jump several feet. Its sandy fur color allows it to blend in with its environment. Its ability to obtain water from seeds means the kangaroo rat never actually has to drink liquid water. Therefore, the correct answer is A.

54. D: This food web indicates that grasshoppers eat grass, which means they are herbivores, not carnivores. Since they are not carnivores, they cannot be predators. Since grasshoppers cannot make their own food, they are not producers. Therefore, the correct answer is D.

How to Overcome Test Anxiety

Just the thought of taking a test is enough to make most people a little nervous. A test is an important event that can have a long-term impact on your future, so it's important to take it seriously and it's natural to feel anxious about performing well. But just because anxiety is normal, that doesn't mean that it's helpful in test taking, or that you should simply accept it as part of your life. Anxiety can have a variety of effects. These effects can be mild, like making you feel slightly nervous, or severe, like blocking your ability to focus or remember even a simple detail.

If you experience test anxiety—whether severe or mild—it's important to know how to beat it. To discover this, first you need to understand what causes test anxiety.

Causes of Test Anxiety

While we often think of anxiety as an uncontrollable emotional state, it can actually be caused by simple, practical things. One of the most common causes of test anxiety is that a person does not feel adequately prepared for their test. This feeling can be the result of many different issues such as poor study habits or lack of organization, but the most common culprit is time management. Starting to study too late, failing to organize your study time to cover all of the material, or being distracted while you study will mean that you're not well prepared for the test. This may lead to cramming the night before, which will cause you to be physically and mentally exhausted for the test. Poor time management also contributes to feelings of stress, fear, and hopelessness as you realize you are not well prepared but don't know what to do about it.

Other times, test anxiety is not related to your preparation for the test but comes from unresolved fear. This may be a past failure on a test, or poor performance on tests in general. It may come from comparing yourself to others who seem to be performing better or from the stress of living up to expectations. Anxiety may be driven by fears of the future—how failure on this test would affect your educational and career goals. These fears are often completely irrational, but they can still negatively impact your test performance.

Elements of Test Anxiety

As mentioned earlier, test anxiety is considered to be an emotional state, but it has physical and mental components as well. Sometimes you may not even realize that you are suffering from test anxiety until you notice the physical symptoms. These can include trembling hands, rapid heartbeat, sweating, nausea, and tense muscles. Extreme anxiety may lead to fainting or vomiting. Obviously, any of these symptoms can have a negative impact on testing. It is important to recognize them as soon as they begin to occur so that you can address the problem before it damages your performance.

The mental components of test anxiety include trouble focusing and inability to remember learned information. During a test, your mind is on high alert, which can help you recall information and stay focused for an extended period of time. However, anxiety interferes with your mind's natural processes, causing you to blank out, even on the questions you know well. The strain of testing during anxiety makes it difficult to stay focused, especially on a test that may take several hours. Extreme anxiety can take a huge mental toll, making it difficult not only to recall test information but even to understand the test questions or pull your thoughts together.

Effects of Test Anxiety

Test anxiety is like a disease—if left untreated, it will get progressively worse. Anxiety leads to poor performance, and this reinforces the feelings of fear and failure, which in turn lead to poor performances on subsequent tests. It can grow from a mild nervousness to a crippling condition. If allowed to progress, test anxiety can have a big impact on your schooling, and consequently on your future.

Test anxiety can spread to other parts of your life. Anxiety on tests can become anxiety in any stressful situation, and blanking on a test can turn into panicking in a job situation. But fortunately, you don't have to let anxiety rule your testing and determine your grades. There are a number of relatively simple steps you can take to move past anxiety and function normally on a test and in the rest of life.

Physical Steps for Beating Test Anxiety

While test anxiety is a serious problem, the good news is that it can be overcome. It doesn't have to control your ability to think and remember information. While it may take time, you can begin taking steps today to beat anxiety.

Just as your first hint that you may be struggling with anxiety comes from the physical symptoms, the first step to treating it is also physical. Rest is crucial for having a clear, strong mind. If you are tired, it is much easier to give in to anxiety. But if you establish good sleep habits, your body and mind will be ready to perform optimally, without the strain of exhaustion. Additionally, sleeping well helps you to retain information better, so you're more likely to recall the answers when you see the test questions.

Getting good sleep means more than going to bed on time. It's important to allow your brain time to relax. Take study breaks from time to time so it doesn't get overworked, and don't study right before bed. Take time to rest your mind before trying to rest your body, or you may find it difficult to fall asleep.

Along with sleep, other aspects of physical health are important in preparing for a test. Good nutrition is vital for good brain function. Sugary foods and drinks may give a burst of energy but this burst is followed by a crash, both physically and emotionally. Instead, fuel your body with protein and vitamin-rich foods.

Also, drink plenty of water. Dehydration can lead to headaches and exhaustion, especially if your brain is already under stress from the rigors of the test. Particularly if your test is a long one, drink water during the breaks. And if possible, take an energy-boosting snack to eat between sections.

Along with sleep and diet, a third important part of physical health is exercise. Maintaining a steady workout schedule is helpful, but even taking 5-minute study breaks to walk can help get your blood pumping faster and clear your head. Exercise also releases endorphins, which contribute to a positive feeling and can help combat test anxiety.

When you nurture your physical health, you are also contributing to your mental health. If your body is healthy, your mind is much more likely to be healthy as well. So take time to rest, nourish your body with healthy food and water, and get moving as much as possible. Taking these physical steps will make you stronger and more able to take the mental steps necessary to overcome test anxiety.

Mental Steps for Beating Test Anxiety

Working on the mental side of test anxiety can be more challenging, but as with the physical side, there are clear steps you can take to overcome it. As mentioned earlier, test anxiety often stems from lack of preparation, so the obvious solution is to prepare for the test. Effective studying may be the most important weapon you have for beating test anxiety, but you can and should employ several other mental tools to combat fear.

First, boost your confidence by reminding yourself of past success—tests or projects that you aced. If you're putting as much effort into preparing for this test as you did for those, there's no reason you should expect to fail here. Work hard to prepare; then trust your preparation.

Second, surround yourself with encouraging people. It can be helpful to find a study group, but be sure that the people you're around will encourage a positive attitude. If you spend time with others who are anxious or cynical, this will only contribute to your own anxiety. Look for others who are motivated to study hard from a desire to succeed, not from a fear of failure.

Third, reward yourself. A test is physically and mentally tiring, even without anxiety, and it can be helpful to have something to look forward to. Plan an activity following the test, regardless of the outcome, such as going to a movie or getting ice cream.

When you are taking the test, if you find yourself beginning to feel anxious, remind yourself that you know the material. Visualize successfully completing the test. Then take a few deep, relaxing breaths and return to it. Work through the questions carefully but with confidence, knowing that you are capable of succeeding.

Developing a healthy mental approach to test taking will also aid in other areas of life. Test anxiety affects more than just the actual test—it can be damaging to your mental health and even contribute to depression. It's important to beat test anxiety before it becomes a problem for more than testing.

Study Strategy

Being prepared for the test is necessary to combat anxiety, but what does being prepared look like? You may study for hours on end and still not feel prepared. What you need is a strategy for test prep. The next few pages outline our recommended steps to help you plan out and conquer the challenge of preparation.

Step 1: Scope Out the Test

Learn everything you can about the format (multiple choice, essay, etc.) and what will be on the test. Gather any study materials, course outlines, or sample exams that may be available. Not only will this help you to prepare, but knowing what to expect can help to alleviate test anxiety.

Step 2: Map Out the Material

Look through the textbook or study guide and make note of how many chapters or sections it has. Then divide these over the time you have. For example, if a book has 15 chapters and you have five days to study, you need to cover three chapters each day. Even better, if you have the time, leave an extra day at the end for overall review after you have gone through the material in depth.

If time is limited, you may need to prioritize the material. Look through it and make note of which sections you think you already have a good grasp on, and which need review. While you are studying, skim quickly through the familiar sections and take more time on the challenging parts.

Write out your plan so you don't get lost as you go. Having a written plan also helps you feel more in control of the study, so anxiety is less likely to arise from feeling overwhelmed at the amount to cover.

Step 3: Gather Your Tools

Decide what study method works best for you. Do you prefer to highlight in the book as you study and then go back over the highlighted portions? Or do you type out notes of the important information? Or is it helpful to make flashcards that you can carry with you? Assemble the pens, index cards, highlighters, post-it notes, and any other materials you may need so you won't be distracted by getting up to find things while you study.

If you're having a hard time retaining the information or organizing your notes, experiment with different methods. For example, try color-coding by subject with colored pens, highlighters, or post-it notes. If you learn better by hearing, try recording yourself reading your notes so you can listen while in the car, working out, or simply sitting at your desk. Ask a friend to quiz you from your flashcards, or try teaching someone the material to solidify it in your mind.

Step 4: Create Your Environment

It's important to avoid distractions while you study. This includes both the obvious distractions like visitors and the subtle distractions like an uncomfortable chair (or a too-comfortable couch that makes you want to fall asleep). Set up the best study environment possible: good lighting and a comfortable work area. If background music helps you focus, you may want to turn it on, but otherwise keep the room quiet. If you are using a computer to take notes, be sure you don't have any other windows open, especially applications like social media, games, or anything else that could distract you. Silence your phone and turn off notifications. Be sure to keep water close by so you stay hydrated while you study (but avoid unhealthy drinks and snacks).

Also, take into account the best time of day to study. Are you freshest first thing in the morning? Try to set aside some time then to work through the material. Is your mind clearer in the afternoon or evening? Schedule your study session then. Another method is to study at the same time of day that you will take the test, so that your brain gets used to working on the material at that time and will be ready to focus at test time.

Step 5: Study!

Once you have done all the study preparation, it's time to settle into the actual studying. Sit down, take a few moments to settle your mind so you can focus, and begin to follow your study plan. Don't give in to distractions or let yourself procrastinate. This is your time to prepare so you'll be ready to fearlessly approach the test. Make the most of the time and stay focused.

Of course, you don't want to burn out. If you study too long you may find that you're not retaining the information very well. Take regular study breaks. For example, taking five minutes out of every hour to walk briskly, breathing deeply and swinging your arms, can help your mind stay fresh.

As you get to the end of each chapter or section, it's a good idea to do a quick review. Remind yourself of what you learned and work on any difficult parts. When you feel that you've mastered the material, move on to the next part. At the end of your study session, briefly skim through your notes again.

But while review is helpful, cramming last minute is NOT. If at all possible, work ahead so that you won't need to fit all your study into the last day. Cramming overloads your brain with more information than it can process and retain, and your tired mind may struggle to recall even previously learned information when it is overwhelmed with last-minute study. Also, the urgent nature of cramming and the stress placed on your brain contribute to anxiety. You'll be more likely to go to the test feeling unprepared and having trouble thinking clearly.

So don't cram, and don't stay up late before the test, even just to review your notes at a leisurely pace. Your brain needs rest more than it needs to go over the information again. In fact, plan to finish your studies by noon or early afternoon the day before the test. Give your brain the rest of the day to relax or focus on other things, and get a good night's sleep. Then you will be fresh for the test and better able to recall what you've studied.

Step 6: Take a Practice Test

Many courses offer sample tests, either online or in the study materials. This is an excellent resource to check whether you have mastered the material, as well as to prepare for the test format and environment.

Check the test format ahead of time: the number of questions, the type (multiple choice, free response, etc.), and the time limit. Then create a plan for working through them. For example, if you have 30 minutes to take a 60-question test, your limit is 30 seconds per question. Spend less time on the questions you know well so that you can take more time on the difficult ones.

If you have time to take several practice tests, take the first one open book, with no time limit. Work through the questions at your own pace and make sure you fully understand them. Gradually work up to taking a test under test conditions: sit at a desk with all study materials put away and set a timer. Pace yourself to make sure you finish the test with time to spare and go back to check your answers if you have time.

After each test, check your answers. On the questions you missed, be sure you understand why you missed them. Did you misread the question (tests can use tricky wording)? Did you forget the information? Or was it something you hadn't learned? Go back and study any shaky areas that the practice tests reveal.

Taking these tests not only helps with your grade, but also aids in combating test anxiety. If you're already used to the test conditions, you're less likely to worry about it, and working through tests until you're scoring well gives you a confidence boost. Go through the practice tests until you feel comfortable, and then you can go into the test knowing that you're ready for it.

Test Tips

On test day, you should be confident, knowing that you've prepared well and are ready to answer the questions. But aside from preparation, there are several test day strategies you can employ to maximize your performance.

First, as stated before, get a good night's sleep the night before the test (and for several nights before that, if possible). Go into the test with a fresh, alert mind rather than staying up late to study.

Try not to change too much about your normal routine on the day of the test. It's important to eat a nutritious breakfast, but if you normally don't eat breakfast at all, consider eating just a protein bar. If you're a coffee drinker, go ahead and have your normal coffee. Just make sure you time it so that the caffeine doesn't wear off right in the middle of your test. Avoid sugary beverages, and drink enough water to stay hydrated but not so much that you need a restroom break 10 minutes into the test. If your test isn't first thing in the morning, consider going for a walk or doing a light workout before the test to get your blood flowing.

Allow yourself enough time to get ready, and leave for the test with plenty of time to spare so you won't have the anxiety of scrambling to arrive in time. Another reason to be early is to select a good seat. It's helpful to sit away from doors and windows, which can be distracting. Find a good seat, get out your supplies, and settle your mind before the test begins.

When the test begins, start by going over the instructions carefully, even if you already know what to expect. Make sure you avoid any careless mistakes by following the directions.

Then begin working through the questions, pacing yourself as you've practiced. If you're not sure on an answer, don't spend too much time on it, and don't let it shake your confidence. Either skip it and come back later, or eliminate as many wrong answers as possible and guess among the remaining ones. Don't dwell on these questions as you continue—put them out of your mind and focus on what lies ahead.

Be sure to read all of the answer choices, even if you're sure the first one is the right answer. Sometimes you'll find a better one if you keep reading. But don't second-guess yourself if you do immediately know the answer. Your gut instinct is usually right. Don't let test anxiety rob you of the information you know.

If you have time at the end of the test (and if the test format allows), go back and review your answers. Be cautious about changing any, since your first instinct tends to be correct, but make sure you didn't misread any of the questions or accidentally mark the wrong answer choice. Look over any you skipped and make an educated guess.

At the end, leave the test feeling confident. You've done your best, so don't waste time worrying about your performance or wishing you could change anything. Instead, celebrate the successful completion of this test. And finally, use this test to learn how to deal with anxiety even better next time.

Review Video: Test Anxiety
Visit mometrix.com/academy and enter code: 100340

Important Qualification

Not all anxiety is created equal. If your test anxiety is causing major issues in your life beyond the classroom or testing center, or if you are experiencing troubling physical symptoms related to your anxiety, it may be a sign of a serious physiological or psychological condition. If this sounds like your situation, we strongly encourage you to seek professional help.

Online Resources

Due to our efforts to try to keep this book to a manageable length, we've created a link that will give you access to all of your online resources:

mometrix.com/resources719/ssreglivingenv

It's Your Moment, Let's Celebrate It!

Share your story @mometrixtestpreparation